Give a F**k

A brief inventory of ways in which you can

FELICITY MORSE

Michael O'Mara Books Limited

First published in Great Britain in 2018 by
Michael O'Mara Books Limited
9 Lion Yard
Tremadoc Road
London SW4 7NQ

A CIP catalogue record for this book
is available from the British Library.

Papers used by Michael O'Mara Books Limited are natural,
recyclable products made from wood grown in sustainable forests.
The manufacturing processes conform to the environmental
regulations of the country of origin.

ISBN: 978-1-78243-919-6 in hardback print format
ISBN: 978-1-78243-952-3 in ebook format

1 2 3 4 5 6 7 8 9 10

Cover design by Ana Bjezancevic
Printed and bound by CPI Group (UK) Ltd, Croydon, CR0 4YY

www.mombooks.com

CONTENTS

A BATTLE OF F**KS

Here's the truth: there are times when being a sensitive, caring human being sucks. This world can be a difficult place to navigate, and if you not only feel all of its pain, but want to change it for the better, then it's easy to become overwhelmed; to burn out, or even check out altogether.

Whether we're aware of it or not, most of us are engaged in a philosophical struggle as we go about our daily lives. It is a fight I have come to see as 'a battle of f★★ks'. Forget 'to be or not to be' – in this golden age of interconnected agitation, post Trump, post Brexit, with so many overwhelming demands on our attention, the existential question we face is whether or not to give an actual f★★k.

It's a question I've sat with for a long time. Working in news for the best part of the last decade, first as a journalist, then as a social-media producer and finally as an editor, my daily diet was once the world's calamities. There were cheery stories, too, of course, but it is the terrible ones that are burnt on my mind: the distressing images and footage; humanity facing unimaginable pain and conflict. Empathy is unavoidable – and exhausting. There comes a point where caring feels just too much.

So I understand if in this battle, you'd rather just say 'F★★k it!' and withdraw into your own comfortable little sphere, murmuring only a cursory 'Isn't it terrible?' at dinner parties. A life where all you really give a f★★k about is reclining on the sofa with a large glass of wine and forgetting about the world's woes, because what could you do about them anyway?

Perhaps this isn't you, but you know of someone a bit like this, though their 'f★★k it' attitude might be dressed a bit differently, in smug pseudo-spiritual garb. You'll identify these folk by their complacent virtue-signalling smile, their faraway look while you try and engage them with the world, only to be advised that 'letting go' or 'taking life less seriously' is the way forward. It's not that I'm unaware of the spiritual benefits of 'surrender'; it's just that this meditative attitude – though wonderful while 'omming' on the mountaintop – is not much use to those of us who live down below in the marketplace and are continually aware of the utter state of things. Letting go is only the first part of any process – we actually need to pick the important stuff back up again and learn how to care about it so that things move and change.

We are part of this world – it affects *us* and we affect *it* – it is inevitable that we care: it is natural and it is right. We're challenged by the difficulty of how to do this without ending up enrolling as a member of another passionate tribe – the worrier cadets – a bunch made inactive by the sheer scale of their concern about everything. They aren't much fun to be around, and their hyperactive cousins, sometimes admirable project managers, can be equally annoying in their evangelism.

You may or may not recognize yourself among some of these stereotypes. In reality, most of us tend to switch sides fairly regularly, depending on how overwhelmed, irritated or exhausted we feel. Neither way quite fits the demands of modern life, so the majority of us ping-pong between the two, watching our newsfeeds, doing overtime at work and occasionally becoming imbued with a sense of injustice and purpose. Until it all gets too much. Then we become wired and tired and pop off for a lie-down, that glass of wine, or sign up for a yoga class. We become rested and then begin to care again, and so the cycle continues.

At some point, even the cycle itself becomes ennui-inducing, and we slowly disengage altogether, living a smaller, more convenient life. Then we aren't even challenged by the discomfort of what to give a f★★k about, as everything has been arranged to be wonderfully comfortable. We haven't found the answer, so we stop even asking the question, dismissing the activity as worthless.

I have joyfully, miserably, painfully, energetically, exhaustedly tried to live my life in all of these arrangements. I have repeatedly floundered and f★★ked up; clawed my way back up to the top of the cliff edge, humiliated but fighting, only to be knocked out by yet another falling boulder (this was an emotional battle – I'm actually not very athletic). In 2015, I reached rock bottom. There wasn't anything dramatic that took me there. I wish there had been; that would have been a good story to tell. It was just the culmination of a thousand little, emotional mosquito-bites that I finally woke up to and decided that I couldn't live with any more.

Finding myself in this unbearable-seeming spot, I had to do something about it. I did a lot of unhelpful and unhealthy things for some time before I started becoming interested in personal-development programmes, enrolling on a number of courses; a process that led me to become a life coach alongside writing. As part of this, I discovered that in the battle of f★★ks, there is a middle way – that you can really care about the important stuff without losing your mind.

You'll know if you've met someone who truly 'cares'; just by talking to them you feel inspired, energetic – suddenly everything feels charged with possibility. It's contagious. Who wouldn't want to be that type of person?

Honing our ability to be caring and curious honours our time here on earth and gives our lives meaning. It makes the world a better place, too. Being conscious of our own existence, staying present with our experiences, and learning about the world in such a way that it happens for us, not to us, is a transformative process.

Like anything worthwhile, it's easier saying it than doing it. But it's all about the doing. See, proper caring is actually a practice. Think of it like a muscle. And as with all training, you need to start small to avoid getting whacked. Lots of us are starting too big with our give-a-f★★k muscle – picking up the 40 kg weight (say, for example, starvation in Africa) – and then deciding it's too heavy for us because we couldn't pick it up successfully. We become disillusioned.

Or perhaps we soldier on regardless, but ultimately pretty pointlessly. How many people do you know who are campaigning for a cause when you feel their attention would be better directed closer to home?

Many of us have also picked up the habit of only really paying attention to the things we are strongly for or against. We give a lot of thought to the things that we hate or annoy us: that woman who won't shut up at work, or the bus replacement service, or the way our partner always leaves the seat up/down. Then we forget about our lovely colleague who always makes our coffee just right, and the weather is not too bad either and aren't the colours of that tree's leaves rather beautiful? Conversely, only focusing on things we love makes us avoidant, turning our attention away from our fears, confrontation, anything that threatens us, telling ourselves and people around us that we 'don't really give a f★★k'.

Think about what's behind not caring. Perhaps spouting provocatively on social media, for example, is exposing that what you *really* long for is human connection. Maybe complaining about your job is a hidden way of saying that you just want to feel fulfilled? We can use what we *don't want* to show us what we do want. Underneath anger often lies fear, and below fear there is usually something we love that we are trying to protect. Clearing surface-obstacles and finding out what we truly care about allows us to get in touch with ourselves.

Admitting you care is a scary mini-rebellion. People think admitting to your fears is hard, but often it's actually expressing what you want or need that's the most challenging and courageous part. Caring is hard. But if you fail at first, don't worry. This journey you're going on is not about beating up on yourself – it's about embracing things and discovering yourself, and doing it with care.

I'm a BIG proponent of giving a f★★k. I firmly believe that it not only empowers you, it empowers your family, your community and, if you do it right, well – the sky's the limit.

What I've learnt so far has been transformative when it comes to my own mental health, my happiness, my relationships, my community – and my power to effect change in the wider world. I hope, even if just a little, that this book will bring some of that transformation your way.

Commit to caring and the possibility of making a positive difference in this chaotic world opens right up. When you align with your values, the things you care about, you not only discover more about yourself, you also reclaim your purpose and naturally discover where your true desire lies.

Caring involves being interested, being curious, in all aspects of life. About directing your attention, embracing the pleasant and the unpleasant, and considering what it gives you and what you can do.

Consider me your give a f★★k personal trainer.

Felicity Morse

Yourself

GIVE A F**K ABOUT YOURSELF

It's not selfish to care about yourself. In fact it's more narrow-minded not to. The world needs you fully alive, awake, happy and nourished, and for that you need to first and foremost give a f★★k about you.

This means fostering a deep acceptance, love and care for yourself, and making sure you make enough space in your life for your vital needs. The demands of your body, your mind, your heart. How else will you learn how to comfort others, if you don't even know how to gracefully attend to the requests of your own sweet self?

There appears to be current confusion in the media between self-care and 'pampering', with the concept of 'self-care' seemingly used to sell a lot of often expensive products or experiences. Self-care is not (just) about getting a pedicure, a massage or perfect skin forever; it's more fundamental than that. It's an attitude towards oneself that says: 'I deserve to be here … I may be flawed, I may be fallible, but I'm just like everyone else, and I deserve to take up space on this planet.' Lovely though it is, there is no amount of pampering that can make up for a belief that you're worthless; that there is something wrong with you; that you're a f★★k-up or undeserving of love – even your own.

If you have these negative beliefs about yourself, they can be intensely painful (believe me, I've been there), but in truth they are a bit arrogant, too. What makes you so awful, different and detestable compared with the rest of the human race? What's so special about you that makes you any less deserving of living on this planet? Nurturing a kinder attitude towards ourselves doesn't happen overnight. Sometimes we need a template to help us get there, which is what this section hopes to provide. Self-care is an attitude, but it's also reflected in our behaviour. When you value yourself, you respect your body and your mind, attending to their needs and what gives them pleasure with all the loving kindness that lives inside of you. You do this no matter what sort of day you've had – or how much you've f★★ked up. You do this because you know you have intrinsic value as a human, and you don't need to do a bunch of things before you can allow yourself to be happy. It was French philosopher Pierre Teilhard de Chardin, who said: 'We are not human beings having a *spiritual* experience. We are spiritual beings having a human experience.'[1]

Caring about yourself is a constantly evolving process – it's not that you have to 'complete' self-love before you can interact with the world. All your experiences in relationships and community can act as practice to help you love yourself. Some people think that the way we see the world reflects how we relate with ourselves. If there are parts of ourselves we have abandoned or rejected, we will judge and become intolerant of them in others. If we are angry at ourselves, we become angry with the world. Similarly, the things we admire in others are qualities we recognize in ourselves, but may not have acknowledged yet – though they are latent within us. Giving a f★★k about yourself in this way is a process of reclaiming the greatness within you and displaying it in your own unique way.

The headings throughout this book are intended to help give you a structure from which, if self-love is still a work in progress, you have a better springboard to get there. Just the willingness to live this way is a loving act in itself. Adopting the behaviours and thinking suggested have helped me remember in darker times that actually I'm pretty nice and worth looking after. I hope now that I've remembered I can help you remember your awesomeness, too. Then, when you see someone struggling, you can do the same for them.

ABOUT RIGHT NOW

Checking in with the present moment regularly is as good as any relaxation retreat on the market. Forget colonic irrigation in the Caribbean: the 'right now' is an energetic pit-stop, and it's a trampoline for the future. If you can face it and be in it – honestly and objectively – then it helps you to set your compass effectively towards where you want to be.

It's fun getting so excited about the future (I call these moments of high energy 'possibility parties') that you sprint towards the destination, fixated on a fantasy. But it doesn't always work if you ignore reality as it is. A map is simply a pretty picture if you can't plot where you are on it accurately.

Trust me, I know.

Some Saturday mornings, while I'm sipping my first cup of coffee, I'm filled with a very strong sense that I might just be able to save the world. I'm post-lie in, there's sunshine streaming through the blinds and the entire weekend sprawls before me. Clear, energized and imbued with my own brilliance, I want to use my (God-given) talents to serve the world.

I could bake a show-stopping cake, begin a community cook-out project. I might get invited on the news, winning wide acclaim. I could pitch my philosophy to international thought leaders. I might start a movement; I could write an erudite and witty Facebook post about it – I bet it would go viral. Gosh, I could end up running for office. My power would be limitless. I bet I could even clean the bathroom.

Fast-forward forty-five minutes. Bleach slowly slugs its way out of an overturned bottle onto the bathroom floor. Kitchen roll is everywhere. The smoke alarm is going off due to the burning cake. The dog has used the brief interlude in which I extinguished the flaming, jam sponge to steal a used tampon from the garbage can.

As I chase him, the belt loops of my dressing gown get hooked onto the kitchen door handle and I fall into a tangled heap. Still attached to the kitchen door, I check social media. Approximately five people have liked the inspirational quote I posted on Facebook. Over in the hallway, the dog is enthusiastically eating the used feminine hygiene product. Le sigh.

Forget saving the world – it is questionable whether I can even save myself.

You might be fortunate enough to never have found yourself in this exact scenario, but most of us can relate to a situation where we started a few different things, full of good intentions, but forgot to factor in the reality part. Things didn't pan out as expected. Other people got involved. Circumstances started competing for our attention. We began feeling like we were spinning lots of plates. If our minds were internet browsers, we'd have thirty-five different tabs open simultaneously, and maybe an annoying pop-up video in the bottom right-hand corner.

It's tempting to say 'F★★k it', walk away, switch off. Give up on what you want and give up doing anything to get it. Say you're not good enough, the world is f★★ked up and it's hopeless.

Returning to the right now is the antidote to that.

When my mind starts spinning out, I bring myself back to the present. Land myself, consciously, in my body and in my mind, in what is going on and how I am feeling right now. Some people check into a luxury hotel to relax; I check in with myself, right there in the moment (because not only am I a smartarse, I'm also a cheapskate).

So, before you get any further, just stop for a second and

make friends with where you are and what's going on for you right now, and just appreciate it for what it is.

- *Take a deep breath, in through your nose and out through your mouth. Acknowledge that it might feel uncomfortable to slow down. Sit with that feeling. It's okay. It's a sign that now is the perfect time to check in with yourself and the right now.*
- *Can you let the skin on your face relax? Let your tongue lie thick and heavy in your mouth? Have your shoulders sunk down? Is your belly relaxed?*
- *Now begin to notice. Start with three things you can see. They can be mundane: this book, that chair, the window in front of you.*
- *Press your index finger and thumb together as you name them under your breath.*
- *Then focus your attention a little more. Notice three things you can hear. It might be traffic. Or birdsong in the distance. The sky might be grumbling; perhaps you can hear wind and rain. Maybe people are talking – there's a low-level murmur. Listen.*
- *Press your middle finger and thumb together as you name them under your breath.*
- *Finally, notice three twhings you can feel. Maybe the texture of the book under your fingers. Or the feeling of whatever you are sitting or lying on. Perhaps it's the feeling of your feet on the ground, in your shoes, or the air on your face.*

● *Press your ring finger and thumb together as you silently name what you can feel.*

You can do this exercise – three things you can see, three things you can hear, three things you can feel – every time stuff starts to feel too much.

A lot of us spend our days doing two or three things at once while half-living an imagined version of the future and occasionally analysing the past. That's a lot of mental effort expended on fighting reality. Living in the right now from time to time saves energy, freeing up more headspace – and with it more concentration.

We can harness the extra attention to refocus on what we really want and what is the best way to get there, taking the complexities of the current situation into account. Or maybe it turns out that without all the extra noise, the right now is actually pretty great.

Forcing the future ends in failure

We all want things. However, sometimes we get so fixated on the 'how' and the 'what' – especially if a certain blueprint was successful in the past or has proved fruitful for others – that we end up missing brilliant opportunities.

Blockbuster's CEO passed up the chance to buy Netflix for $50million. Would Blockbuster have gone bust if he'd taken a moment to check in with what was going on in the right now with changing technologies?

It's not just businesses that fall victim to this kind of thinking. A lot of us become unwilling to adapt to changing circumstances. A detailed plan can quickly turn into tunnel vision. We become over-attached not just to what we want to happen, but to exactly how that thing is going to happen and what it's going to look like. I call it trying to force the future.

It's easy to say that Blockbuster should have seen it coming, but I know in more than one situation I've been so absorbed in what I think should happen, or what I desperately want to happen, that I've missed what actually was happening. This result was more mess and pain than needed to be.

It used to happen to me often when I was dating. The evidence was all there that we weren't right for each other, but I was so fixated on what I wanted to happen that I ignored all the signs, getting off on my bridal-suite fairy tale of what our future could hold. Sure, it was too uncomfortable to confront the truth of the situation and realize I wasn't happy, but it was even messier to wake up nine months down the line in crisis about it.

Our minds can attend to 126 pieces of information per second[2] – there's always more we can pay attention to in the right now.

I'm not suggesting you should just quit if a situation or a relationship isn't perfect right away. I'm saying you have to tackle 'what is' rather than what you want it to be in order to move forward. This applies to so many things. We don't face the right now of our finances. We spend time in friendships that have gone stale or make us feel bad. We ignore the health of our bodies and stick for years moaning about a job, just hoping it will change. We resist the right now because it's painful or it doesn't feel like it's where we want to be. Yet when we can't accept the situation as it truly is, we create drama for ourselves and others in the long term.

There's also the chance that, maybe, once we slow down and come into the now, once we stop trying to get anywhere at all and accept the situation as it is, we find out that where we are feels pretty damn good and we could stop and think about just appreciating that for a minute?

Snakes and ladders

'Right now' isn't always rosy. Accepting 'what is' is especially bruising if, like me, you prefer feeling as though you are constantly making progress. I'm not sure who first gave me the idea that from birth to death there should be some sense of continual forward movement, but if I do meet the aforementioned individual I shall tell them I feel deeply misled.

Life feels more like a game of snakes and ladders: sometimes you roll the dice and move forward steadily; at other times, you roll a few ladders and breakthroughs happen rapidly. Being in the right now at that point is easy. Hurrah!

Then, perhaps just as you feel you're on a winning streak,

right up ahead, you roll a snake and slink down a few places. Then you meet another snake, and then another, and before you know it, it feels like you're almost back at the beginning, way out on your own. If that's your right now, I understand. I've been there.

At those times, remember that *all we have* is the present moment, and that there are always more resources available to you than you think – both on the outside and on the inside – once you've wiped the tears away.

This moment matters

Being present in the right now, and allowing yourself to feel what is going on for you in the moment you are in, is in itself an act of bravery. We're talking about confronting the brutal facts of life now, folks – and choosing to go on in spite of that, because you are willing to believe that there's something better and that you will get there in the end.

Even if right now is uncomfortable, it matters – perhaps even more so. How did you end up here? What needs to change? What can you learn from this moment?

Hold in your heart the knowledge that it's not always possible or necessary to be aware of the exact route you're taking somewhere – you can still be victorious. Life is not always linear. Who am I to say that getting a snake and falling down right now won't mean I'll end up on a long ladder in a few rolls? Maybe if I didn't roll a snake, I wouldn't be able to climb that long ladder? This moment will matter in ways you can't imagine yet.

If you've rolled a snake recently, here's what I do. I confront the present reality, with its lipstick and eyeliner off, then I look around and ask myself what the next thing I could do right now to move me forward might be. And I roll the dice. And after I've moved forward a few places, I look around, take stock and ask myself what the next right step might be. It doesn't all have to happen on a sunny Saturday morning.

Then, step by step, you arrive where you want to be – sometimes sooner than you expected.

That's the funny thing about sustainable change. It doesn't look quite the way we expect. Sometimes, it doesn't feel like you're moving at all, which can be frustrating if, like me, you love seeing progress.

At those times I think of it like a flower blooming. You don't notice growth taking place, until suddenly you walk past a tree on your road and you're like 'Wow, the blossom is out'. As if it happened suddenly, all in one fell swoop. But really it's been lots of things coming together slowly, step by tiny step, imperceptibly, until then magic happens.

Acknowledge the good stuff

When we're checking in with the present it's also important to take stock of all the good things we have received and achieved. Often, we discount them in favour of focusing on an obstacle, but without acknowledging the solid bits underneath and behind us, we have no foundation from which we can climb mountains. Plus, half the fun is how you get there – life does not need to be a relentless, joyless race towards some spurious notion of success. You are allowed to enjoy life, even if you haven't done everything on your to-do list.

Sometimes when I'm checking in with right now, and feel like at this moment my reality is brutal, I make a list. I write 'Right Now' at the top, then create two columns underneath. Under one column I write 'Good Things' and in the other column I write 'Bad Things'.

Sometimes, I just start the list of Good Things with 'I'm alive'. It's a decent beginning. As Jon Kabat-Zim writes in *Full Catastrophe Living*[3], 'As long as you are breathing, there is more right with you than there is wrong, no matter how ill or how hopeless you may feel.'

None of us knows what will happen tomorrow. Every twenty-four hours that passes, the clock ticks past the exact time of the day that (hopefully far in the future) I will die. Checking in with my 'death anniversary' is something I choose to remember in my most irritable, frustrated moments. This morbid thought is not meant to send you spiralling into bleakness; it's just a gentle reminder to live in the moment. To appreciate what you can, however messy that looks right now.

So yes, this moment matters. It's also all we ever have. The past is gone, the future can rarely be imagined. All that is real is here and now. And if you're willing to pause for a moment and look around, it could be greater than you imagine.

HOW YOU TALK TO YOURSELF

What does it sound like inside your head?

Most of us have an internal commentary chatting away as we go about our daily business. It can be judgemental: 'Those pink leggings make you look like a flamingo.' It can give us pep talks: 'No, don't worry – your outfit is salmon and you look great!' It can muse: 'I wonder if he was put off by your clothes?' It can curse: 'Why are you always stuck walking behind the slowest people in the universe?' Sometimes, mine sounds exactly like my mother: 'Yes, she is dressed badly and so are you, darling – it's why you don't have a boyfriend. Now hurry up and get to work.'

This inner voice differs for each of us. (I hope no one else has the dubious pleasure of hearing my disembodied mum.) Some people think in scattered words – the subconscious fills in the rest (late – bus – twenty-five minutes – work). Pictures – or visual thinking – can sometimes dominate or even decorate the self-talk. We all have a slightly different inner landscape. Getting to know the voices in my head has been a significant part of transforming my mindscape, from something resembling a volcanic Mordor, to more of a luscious and only occasionally rainy forest.

See, somewhere along the way my internal monologue turned on me. The inner coach always driving me on, asking me to do better, became a bully. This self-critic was brutal and destructive to my confidence, spitting the kind of bile that no one in real life would do or dare say to me.

It sounded a bit like this: 'Your stomach looks massive in that – really ugly. People will be repulsed by you. Look at those stains on your teeth. You shouldn't be smoking. It's disgusting. You're disgusting. You have no self-control. Why haven't you done that project you said you'd do? You're useless. You need to do it now. You're not allowed to enjoy anything until you've done it. I bet you can't do it anyway. If you can't do this you're worth nothing.'

Really charming. You can't win either – you tell yourself you can't do something, and at the same time that you have to do something. Living with this voice has at times made me defensive, irritable and unable to relate to people well. I was walking around buried in shame half the time; tight and angry from fighting off the other half. So what was the purpose of this voice? And how could I turn the volume down?

Well, once I tuned in, I realized what was going on. As much as this inner critic made life hard for me, I'd assumed it was what motivated me. If I stopped feeding this bully with worry and attention, I believed I would end up doing nothing and then be proved right by it; if even beating myself up didn't force me into action, then how unproductive would I be if I let it go?

In reality, I was achieving *in spite* of this self-criticism, not *because* of it. And the things I didn't want to do? I still didn't do them – whether the critic dialled up the abuse or not. All that happened was that I felt much worse about them, making myself feel bad. What's the point in that? It was clear that I needed a different way of motivating myself.

At some point I gave this voice a name and character: Mr Peanut – an unbelievable perfectionist. Naming him something silly helped a lot. Sometimes I give him a Scooby Doo-style voice, too. It's hard to take a cartoon dog seriously. Doing this helped distance the critic from me as a person – and it gave me a bit of breathing room to be a human being, and do what I want sometimes, instead of constantly being nagged about what I should do.

After a while, I started to hear another quiet voice that came in response to Mr Peanut. This new voice told me that I could do this, that I was brilliant, that I did have the ability and I would get there in the end. It ended up being much more worthwhile for me to tune into that voice (I've called her Angelica, because she's an absolute godsend) and motivate myself lovingly forward.

Even if you aren't convinced you'd succeed without your inner critic, let me put it this way: if you aren't getting where you want to go in a way that feels good, what's the point? Yes, you might end up changing your circumstances to something apparently richer, better looking, or cleverer – and you might complete that project in record time. My guess, however, is that your success will feel pretty hollow if you've had to flagellate yourself into the ground to get there, hating every minute of it. You can't hate your way into a life that feels good. Trust me, I've tried.

This life is harsh enough without you turning on your own sweet self, too. There are enough battles worth fighting in this world – waging war on yourself is not one of them. Someone will let you know if you've f★★ked up, I promise you.

That leads me to the second reason I put up with Mr Peanut for so long: protection from all those real-life critics. Somewhere deep down, I had this idea that if I could be really mean to myself, then no one would be able to hurt me, because I'd got there first. If I could just pre-empt everything bad about myself I could toughen myself up, or I could change it or hide it before anyone noticed; then I would be safe. This just wasn't true. It actually stopped me from seeing the more immature parts of myself that needed attention.

The less savoury sides of yourself won't come out into the light if your internal landscape is so full of judgement and shame – it's too painful to confront them. Your inner critic just ends up weakening your self-worth to such a low level that you can't cope with hearing or seeing anything else about yourself that might need attention – either from outside or inside. You can end up living a life in retreat – from yourself and the world; all because it's got thorny in your own head.

Adjusting your inner voice is a process. When I'm making lots of changes in my life or doing something new, this voice of self-doubt sometimes shows up again. I think it's just a side of me that gets scared and wants me to shrink back into a place that's more comfortable. Now I speak to my inner voice and say, 'I know you're just trying to protect me, but actually I've got this.' Other times I just say, 'F★★k off, will you? I'm sick of you crowding my brain!'

Some days I wake up and feel so bad I think, 'Wow, it's going to be pretty easy to beat myself up today'. On those days, I make a vow – I say I won't tell myself a single bad thing about myself. It's surprisingly difficult. By the way, this doesn't mean being completely unself-conscious or, to use a well-worn phrase, 'blowing smoke up your arse'; it means committing to reframing situations in a way that serves you and whatever you're trying to do better.

Reframe it

Once upon a time I was a manager. I found myself in a difficult work situation where I kept telling myself I'd done something wrong. Despite doing everything I possibly could, the voice telling me I wasn't good enough kept worrying away. I was running this script (or rather a script was running me) that I couldn't make my team happy and this meant I was a bad manager, they hated me, I was a terrible person, etc., etc. In the end I nixed it by telling myself, 'I am glad I care enough that I keep worrying about this, even though I've done everything I can.' That made the clouds clear in my brain a little.

Love your nasty bits out of existence

Half of working with your inner critic is developing a louder voice to answer it – one that is kind and forgiving. You can see the emergence of your critic as a chance to creatively turn that voice around and cultivate a new voice. You can do this by consciously reframing what you're telling yourself in a positive way. For example, 'I'm too aggressive and masculine' becomes 'Sometimes I come across as defensive, but that's because I'm excitable and really want things to go well'. Or, 'My belly is fat and disgusting' becomes 'I may want to lose weight, but right now I choose to love my soft, enveloping tummy, like a vintage goddess.' Keep on looking for the good side of the thing you are criticizing yourself for – and it gets easier and easier to find.

Note: Be careful that once you identify the voice you don't beat yourself up about beating yourself up – or beat yourself up about beating yourself up about beating yourself up. Mr Peanut is clever that way – he tries to make me feel bad about feeling bad.

Your self-talk transformation

Stand in the mirror – face yourself – and find things to love. Put one hand on your heart and one on your belly to comfort you as you do this.

The most wonderful thing I've discovered about developing a really kind inner voice is that it can't help but come into play when I talk with other people now. It's as if by developing this new compassionate way of relating to myself, suddenly I'm relating to other people in a much more understanding manner, too. That in itself then reaps its own rewards when they beam love back at me. There's a phrase, 'Point one finger at someone else and three fingers come pointing back at you'. Now, when I hear people spouting bile at others, I feel bad for them, knowing that if it sounds that nasty externally, it must sound really mean for them in their mind. Turning this on its head: giving yourself a hug means you can share three more hugs with others.

The challenge really begins when you make a mistake. When you've done something wrong and someone else suggests you're worth less because of it. This is where I choose to separate what I've done from who I am as a person. I tell myself that even though I f★★ked up, I am not a f★★k-up. That thing I did or didn't do might have been bad, but I am not bad. And then, because I want to improve, I look objectively at why I did what I did, what I could have done, and how I could prevent it from happening again. This bettering process is a lot easier to do if every mistake you make doesn't mean you *are* a mistake. Facing up to things you've done wrong is a question of changing the behaviour, rather than having to make some fundamental change to yourself.

Whenever mistakes mean that you put your actual self under threat, you begin to clam up, you get defensive, because looking at what happened, or admitting you did something wrong, means putting your entire being – who you are – on the line. The truth is, you don't need to fix yourself, because you're not broken. But you may need to fix some behaviour and clean up any mess you made because of that behaviour. Looking at things this way empowers you to take charge of your own destiny. Making mistakes becomes a way to make progress rather than 'proof' that your inner critic was right all along.

FEELINGS

Emotions get a bad rap. We say a co-worker is 'sensitive' and wrinkle our noses, as if having feelings is the least desirable thing in the world.

When I ask my coaching clients, 'How do you feel today?', often they'll struggle to reply with anything beyond 'good' or 'stressed'. Using our feeling-sense is so unfamiliar, we can barely identify our own emotions any more. One bold gentleman simply refused to answer the question at all, telling me, 'To be honest, I find emotions a bit wishy-washy.'

I'm British; I get it. But this demonization of feelings does no one any good long term. Feelings themselves do not cause harm – it's how we respond to them that creates such chaos. When we say we are 'too emotional' – we mean we don't like the way we react to having certain feelings.

There's a word for good stress – it was coined by Hungarian endocrinologist (hormone scientist) Hans Selye – '**eustress**' (good) as opposed to 'distress' (bad). There's not an external difference between good or bad stress; it totally depends on and is delineated by, our response.

It's no surprise that so many of us struggle with our reactions to emotions. We are taught to tap them down from a young age: they are dangerous; other people don't like us if we show them. One of the first things we say to a weeping child is 'don't cry'. We get very little chance to practise how to feel well, to hold that emotional energy in our body or release it and direct it wisely.

And so we grow up, numbing and avoiding where we can (bottle of Prosecco after work, anyone?). But suppressing emotions wastes time and energy. It's a bit like pushing a beach ball underwater. Despite a lot of exertion, it inevitably pops up anyway, exploding out of the water with force.

You can't banish emotions. Feelings are part of being human, hard-wired into us for survival. Big powerful emotions (fear, jealousy, anger, even love) will arise in spite of our best efforts.

After a lifetime of anaesthesia, experiencing that much energy is overwhelming. Our society is not set up to support or even tolerate these extreme feelings, either. Much of the time we aren't allowed to share or show them in a stable environment – these emotions are actually taboo.

It's why, when something like anger comes up, we try and get rid of that energy as quickly as possible. We're in such a rush, we're so uncomfortable, we don't always expel it in useful ways. And that's when people get punched in the face.

When someone labels us 'emotional', what they are really saying is: 'I have no idea how to handle my own emotions, let alone yours. Seeing your emotions reminds me of this and it is making me so uncomfortable that I am going to need to blame you for it. It is not personal, it is just that I have no template for interpreting this bodily sensation. I'm not sure what to do and I don't like that. Therefore, right now, I will call you bad.'

I'm not saying you need to go around sharing your feelings with everyone you meet, but you sure as hell need to at least share them with yourself. Oh, and here's another thing: contrary to popular opinion, facing your own emotions and allowing yourself to feel them takes real courage. Anyone who says otherwise is speaking from just one emotion – and that's fear.

I'm not going to lie – emotions can be painful. That's actually okay. It's called growth. Yeah, I know it feels like sh★t. You'll survive though. The truth is, if you don't ever feel f★★ked up, you're probably doing life wrong.

Intense turmoil to one side, there are actually some incredible benefits to cultivating feelings. But first – how to feel without knocking yourself (or someone else) out.

How to feel

One way that emotions show up is as sensations in the body – they each have their own tell-tale footprint and feel a little different for every one of us.

Happiness might show up as a light, expansive feeling in the chest, a relaxation of the skin on the face. Disgust might appear as a sickness in the stomach, a hunching and tenseness in the shoulders. Peaceful might feel like a fanning release across the shoulders, the corners of your mouth turned up, a spacious feeling in your forehead.

It's useful to be able to identify emotions like this. Sensing in this way takes you out of your jumble of thoughts – out of your head and back into your body. Big 'scary' emotions are reduced to a collection of physical sensations – which for me always feels far more manageable. It serves as a reminder to me that I am not my emotions – they shift and move and change.

There's actually no scientific consensus on the definition of emotion. The etymological root of the word emotion is from Latin – 'to move out'. The word 'feeling' comes from the old English, 'felan': to touch or have a sensory experience of; perceive, sense (something).

Separate the thought from the feeling

Focusing on the actual sensations occurring in your body, while noticing whether you have a preference for them or not, allows you to experience whatever you are feeling without getting caught in a thousand different thoughts.

These thoughts often complicate and prolong the emotional experience – one negative thought sparking another negative thought, until the original thing we felt hurt or sad about suddenly appears much worse than it is. Ever had that experience where you begin crying; say about breaking up with someone – and then you start remembering every other past failed relationship and then you begin connecting all the dots and make a wee story for yourself about how you're totally unlovable – and maybe even your parents don't love you – and begin weeping harder and harder? Or you get fired from a job that you didn't want anyway, and then you start thinking you're never going to make any money, and didn't your seventh-grade teacher tell you that and then before you know it, your problem isn't that you don't have a job, it's that you're worthless? Well this method of locating and focusing on the sensations avoids going into that kind of experience.

You can't rationalize your way out of a storm

Separating our emotion from our thought is important because most of the time, we feel a feeling and it's strong and the next step is that we try and rationalize it. It's natural but it's not helpful.

When you try and rationalize it away and it doesn't work, it simply makes you feel like an irrational idiot. Now, not only do you feel bad, you also feel bad about feeling bad.

The other way is even worse: we rationalize our strong feeling by exaggerating the awfulness of the situation to match the depth of our emotional response. Focusing on the physical sensation is a neutral way of going into the feeling, while still allowing its release.

Experiencing strong emotions is sometimes like being

caught in the eye of a storm. And if you're caught in a storm, you don't try and get out of it, you go somewhere safe and ride it out. You can work out what to do later. Have you ever tried to give advice to someone who was having an intense emotional experience? Can they hear it? No. They get annoyed. Don't do it to yourself. Just allow the emotions to come.

Facing it, locating it, asking it, loving it

Here's something you can do alone or with a friend you trust. If you're doing it solo, either write it down, speak it out loud or record it on your phone.

- *Set a timer. Commit to fifteen minutes. This allows you to sink into your emotions, without them feeling overwhelming and endless.*
- *Take two deep breaths, in through the nose and out through the mouth. Start asking yourself the questions:*
- *Question 1: 'How are you feeling right now?'*
- *(Example answer): 'I am feeling angry.'*
- *(Response): 'Thank you.' Give yourself permission to feel this.*

Watch out for thoughts disguised as feelings; these often come with a 'like'. For example, 'I feel like I want to punch my boss.' Remember, stress is not a feeling – it's a reaction to a feeling, or a mixture of feelings.

Tip: If you're struggling or can only come up with 'I feel exhausted', change Question 1 to: 'What feeling are you resisting?'

- *Question 2: 'Where do you feel this in your body?'*
  (Example answers): 'Contraction in my stomach' or 'Heat in my face.'
- *Response: 'Thank you.'*
  Take a moment. Breathe into the sensations.
- *Question 3: 'What does this emotion want to show you?'*
- *(Example answers): 'That one of my boundaries has been crossed' or 'It has brought up a memory.'*
- *Track the feeling back – what triggered it?*
- *Question 4: 'What is this emotion asking for?'*
- *With love, attend to your feeling and ask what it needs. Maybe you need to cry or be hugged. If one of your boundaries has been crossed, you might thank your emotion for letting you know and pledge not to allow that to happen again.*
- *Now give yourself permission to let the feeling go. Say: 'I am letting you go now.'*
- *Visualize this feeling leaving your body, as though it is a cloud heading back up to the sky. If you want, you can even open a window and 'hand' the energy back to the universe.*

For me, not to me

The next time you're under emotional pressure, ask yourself the following: 'How is this happening for me, rather than to me?' Imagine someone has engineered this exact configuration of events to show you something or let you learn something. What is the opportunity here for you to grow and be more powerful?

Truly sensational

Certain emotions are physiologically very similar. Fear and excitement, for example. There's a wonderful experiment described in Ian Robertson's book *The Stress Test* [4] where, halfway across a high, rickety, suspension bridge over a deep canyon, men were stopped by a female research assistant and asked to take part in a study on the effects of scenic attractions on creativity, and if they could write a short story. The same exercise was repeated, with the same assistant, but this time on a sturdy bridge. The men who did the exercise on the rickety bridge wrote stories thick with sexual imagery, and were far more likely to try and contact the research assistant personally afterwards.

The explanation? The men on the bridge were already experiencing the kind of sensations prompted by risk and fear – sweaty palms, increased heart rate – when the pretty research assistant approached them. Some of the men misinterpreted the emotional signals prompted by the height of the bridge as arousal, given the presence of the female assistant. This was not the case for those men who took the test on the sturdier platform.

We can actually use this to our advantage sometimes. If you can interpret anxiety as excitement – as being ready to go – because the physiological symptoms are so similar

– it may actually change how you think and feel about the situation, enabling you to make better choices and take bolder action.

This phenomenon also lies behind one of the major benefits of allowing yourself to feel. So many challenging emotions share overlapping sensations with pleasant emotions. You can't numb one emotion without numbing a whole range. If you start allowing yourself to feel, you might have a more acute experience of grief, sadness, disappointment – but you'll also be able to feel more happiness, joy, contentment and love. It might sometimes be uncomfortable and messy – but messy-beautiful.

Emotions are your 'sherpa'

Some people have an idea of what they think will make them happy – the ideal body shape, the good job, the hefty salary, the nice car, the big house, the romantic relationship. Happiness has taken on a certain form for those people, and they look to achieve those things as their route to it. Actually, most of the time the form is irrelevant – it's the feeling underneath the form that's important: the self-worth, the satisfaction, the intimacy, the feeling of being valued, the love, the sex, the freedom. You can work your way into the grave getting all of the things in the 'form' list and still be utterly miserable. Because those weren't the things you actually wanted; it was the feeling you thought they would provide you with that you craved.

This is important when it comes to feelings, because when you learn to be guided by your emotions you can start making decisions based on what feels good instead of what looks or sounds good, or even what 'rationally' makes sense. If your thoughts are saying one thing and your emotions and body another, you can bet the latter is more truthful. In those situations, it's worth tuning in, and asking why – and what – a certain thing is giving you. In this way, emotions can be thought of as 'energetic information': sensations in our body that can provide important clues for us to get to know ourselves, helping guide us towards a happier life.

STORYTELLING

'Storytelling' has most likely been a big part of your life without you even noticing –and will probably continue thus until you die. It's a stealthy yet powerful, invisible yet omnipresent force in all of our lives.

Storytelling is an innately human urge – we construct narratives to share with each other on such a fundamental scale that it's as instinctual to our nature as drinking water.

From an early age we are read stories by our parents; as babies we are bewitched and soothed by the sounds of language, which as we grow, gradually becomes comprehensible as bedtime stories. Teachers share instructive fables to teach us simple lessons, and of course, we are protected by 'cautionary tales', warning us of the world's perils.

Stories have many functions in our lives – we use them to empathize with different viewpoints and assimilate and absorb knowledge (show me a TED talk that doesn't have at least one story). We use them to make sense of the world, which might be one reason we get so frustrated when certain narratives challenge us with their meaning, or films or books fail to provide a satisfying ending.

Yet more often than not, storytelling is so instinctive to us we aren't always conscious of when and why we do it. That's particularly the case when it comes to the stories we tell about ourselves.

Self-scheming storytellers

As consummate storytellers, we often edit – depending on our audience and medium. We know we do this, and quite often it's so slight and subconscious we wouldn't even call it 'lying'. After all, we wouldn't present the same version of our story to a potential employer as we would to a potential partner on a first date.

Underneath all of this surface storytelling, are the stories we tell ourselves about ourselves. Messages from authority figures, information we receive from our parents, our emotional memories and shared experiences converge to construct a mental narrative about our own lives, our own character, the sort of person we are and the sort we aren't. We tell ourselves stories about who and what we like and dislike, what we are good or bad at, and how people relate to us. Psychologists call these sets of self-perceptions 'self schemes'. I'm going to call them stories.

I call them stories, rather than beliefs or an ethos, to

emphasize that this identity-making process is drawn from a narrative we create for ourselves, a collection of stories that are fluid and far from fixed. There's no right or wrong story – there's simply helpful or unhelpful, interesting or boring. We are scriptwriters here, often unconscious ones, selecting certain events, applying a lens, stripping or saving details, positioning pivotal plot points; characterizing heroes, villains and most importantly, defining a certain role for ourselves.

There is nothing inherently wrong with doing this, provided your stories are healthy, flexible and constructive – that is, they help you feel positive and allow you to get the best out of life.

The problem is, many of our own personal stories don't meet these criteria at all. They say that we've been left, let down or victimized. They focus on being hurt, damaged and abused. That isn't to say that any of these things didn't or won't happen, aren't painful, should be ignored or edited out of the narrative, but if it is only these elements that are selected to play starring roles in your story – while personal power, redemption, love, community and growth are forgotten – then you're left to play out a tragedy, with yourself as the unfortunate protagonist, fated to failure.

Why do we do this? Partly because our brains like to generalize, using the information we've received in the past to decide how to act in certain situations; what to do and useful strategies – otherwise every time we face a situation that is only slightly different from past experiences, we'll feel totally floored.

The problem occurs when we over-generalize, then apply a layer of confirmation bias over the top. We assume that because one person has treated us badly, or one situation turned out a certain way, that all people will treat us badly and all situations will turn out in that way. We use certain circumstances as 'proof' of our flaws and we live this fixed narrative, going about our lives with distorted and even damning stories about ourselves and others, only heeding the data that fits these beliefs. Perhaps that's why they say first impressions count: once we've got a story running, the brain is tempted to ignore, disbelieve or disregard any contrary evidence. Through the power of storytelling, a bad experience becomes a belief that has the power to rule and ruin our life.

For example, the school bully might have teased you for being overweight and other students, also scared of the bully, might have laughed. You were very hurt by this experience which made you feel not only overweight, but also disrespected, unattractive, unloved, and worthless.

You grow up and lose weight, however you still believe that you are unattractive and unlovable because you have this story. Now, when you go on dates, every gesture, statement, joke or question is filtered and analyzed under the lens of 'they probably won't like me'. Your brain becomes conditioned to this process, surveying and selecting only information to confirm this story.

You mistake someone's shy nature as lack of interest and so you don't call them back, even though you might have liked to. When a different date asks to meet up again, you assume it is from pity or boredom, so you feign disinterest and they withdraw. Left with no one, you now make your story about being unattractive again true. Convenient, eh?

Even when all the contrary evidence stacks up, overwhelming the original narrative, the story still needs to be true: you finally meet someone who likes and pursues you. You end up becoming a couple, but deep down you wonder if there is something wrong with them for being with you. Eventually you sabotage the relationship, convinced it could not last anyway, because that would contradict the storyline.

Congratulations, you were right! Once again, your doubts are justified. Your story is true, because you've made it true.

Our stories can become self-fulfilling prophecies – even when they aren't ours. Your self-perception might be inherited from your mother, for example. Adding insult to injury; not only are these stories downgrading your experience of your life, they aren't even yours! Recognising these stories is imperative, because unless you catch them at their root and tear them out, they can derail your life. It's not just about subconsciously confirming them – sometimes they control us because we are desperately fighting to disprove them: scrambling to the top of the corporate ladder because your geography teacher said you would never succeed. Developing an arrogant attitude to refute a deeply entrenched story of worthlessness. That's no good either because these old chestnuts are still there, dictating your life and your choices.

For a long time, I was so hooked on achievement (in reaction to a story that I wasn't 'good enough'). No matter how many accolades I won this story revolved in my head; stronger than the facts, which could never win against a story I had created for myself. Our brains are funny old things, electing to be right rather than happy. The soggy logic is something like this – we might be miserable, but at least we feel in control!

Five steps to rewriting your story

1. *Being ready: the first step to rewriting your stories is being willing to let go of the old ones. You might not be ready yet. Often we need to feel heard, to express our emotions fully and have that validated, before we can work on moving forward. To rewrite our stories, there has to be a decision to stop defining ourselves through hurt or pain, but in order to do that, sometimes we need to delve into that pain, explore it, analyze it and understand it rather than dodging, ignoring or burying it any longer.*

2. *It can be tough to relinquish old stories; to which we cling stubbornly in fear or familiarity. At this juncture, pause: it's time to introduce acceptance. Accept things did not go the way you wanted them to, accept that you would have preferred a different outcome to the situation. Accept that things you were not okay with this, and that not being okay with it is acceptable. Accepting these disappointments can resolve the conflict you feel towards them, removing emotional clutter and freeing up space so that you can reframe the circumstances differently moving forward.*

3. *Identifying an old or unhelpful story: look for place in your*

life where you feel stuck – where you keep repeating the same behaviour, which is not giving you the result you desire. Or maybe look at a part of your life that makes you feel out of control and powerless to change it. Identify something that has happened that cannot be undone and makes you think that now 'your life is terrible', or you feel someone has 'done' something to you. These are indicators that a story is twisting your thoughts or actions and that a rewrite of your narrative would benefit you.

4. *Flesh out the narrative: let's use being cheated on by an ex-partner as an example. It's a situation that lots of people have been in, and it can feel very painful when it happens to you. It doesn't necessarily have to be though – at least not forever. Get a pen and paper for this. It's hard to work with our thoughts when they feel like impenetrable clouds of amorphous negativity. What you aim to create is a neutral description of what happened (challenge yourself to describe the event or situation in the most skeletal way possible) and then strip away every possible meaning. For example, 'A person I had agreed to be in a monogamous relationship with slept with someone else without telling me first'.*

5. *Conclusions. What did you extrapolate from this situation? What were you telling yourself at that time? Example: 'I was hurt. I was betrayed, I couldn't understand why he hadn't told me. I wasn't enough. I didn't understand why I didn't see it coming. I wasn't able to protect myself. I couldn't trust anyone again, I couldn't trust myself. Relationships weren't safe. People aren't to be trusted'.*

6. *Rewriting the story. there are several ways to go about this – different questions and methods will resonate for different people with different stories. Often, there'll be a lightbulb moment, almost like when you look at those optical illusions and you finally see the faces instead of the candlestick, or the old woman instead of the young woman. Other times it takes a bit more work. One therapist asked me, 'If I went out and described your story to 100 different people do you think they would come to the same conclusion as you?' I had to admit that they wouldn't.*

The stories we have about ourselves and the world don't change overnight. Even once we accept rationally that there is the possibility of an altered version of events that might be just as true as the one we're captive to, it takes time to weave stories of growth and empowerment into our conscious experience of the world. One emotional occurance can activate a cluster of stories and in those situations it can be hard to weave a narrative that serves us rather than saddens us. It ultimately requires repetition and practice: ask yourself three questions whenever you're in a place that feels bad:

● *What story am I telling myself here?*
● *Is it serving me?*
● *Could I tell myself anything else that would move me closer to the result I want?*

The process of recognizing, accepting and reframing harmful stories that we may have relied on to make sense of our world for a long time, is a tough practice to master. The hardest part is letting go. Our brains have become so invested in these narratives and interpreted so many events to fit them, that clearing away the detritus obscuring our true self can be disorienting and painful. It's confusing and humbling to realise we're telling ourselves these hurtful things; that we are causing ourselves this pain because of the narrative we're draping all over the event.

Whenever you are tempted to abandon unravelling your stories because it's painful or difficult, imagine these stories as poison ivy wrapping itself around a tree. Left untended, the ivy's vines grow swiftly and imperceptibly, taking more than its share of light and nourishment so subtly and totally, that eventually our poor tree is strangled by the creeper. In this way accepting and feeding a negative narrative weakens us too. All that lives, thrives and flourishes is the story while we are left with nothing but pain.

Choose to cast yourself as a hero instead. You can defend your inner kingdom from these enemies to your well-being by realizing your story and staying vigilant to the desire to falsify 'evidence' of your failings automatically. Enlist a fellow warrior to help you out – my friends call me out when I start relating some negative narrative, nudging me and saying, 'Great story you've got there.' Or, 'Was it completely unbearable? You look like you are still here to me.'

Arm yourself with acceptance, forgiveness, don your

reframing lens, and tell yourself you will overcome these mental monsters. The story isn't over yet, after all.

YOUR BODY

We all live with a creature. A soft, forgiving, but nonetheless perishable creature. This beautiful creature, who was born with us, is unique to us in many ways. It can look after itself most of the time, but does ask us for certain things so that we can both live happily.

We can't exist without this creature, and yet many of us forget it or disrespect it, no matter that this soft animal has our best interests at heart. We treat our creature like an inconvenience, we ignore it until it cries out for attention, and even then we pretend to hear something different.

This creature is our body. We live in a culture that is mean to our creature selves in many ways. That rates it only for what it looks like or what it can do compared with other people. Yet this creature has its own form of wisdom that can't be argued with. It is worth listening to. After all, we don't just live with a creature, we live inside a creature. It's important for us to learn how to work with our creature self if we want to live well and do great things.

Sometimes, it's not a mystery why we feel the way we do when we actually take note of how we treat our bodies. I once went to a therapist for anxiety and insomnia. I was in a bad way – close to falling apart really. I told her all about my failed relationships, how I couldn't make friends. I branched into a long story about how I was in the wrong job and everyone hated me and I was pretty sure I hated everyone, too.

We also talked about my lifestyle. She asked me about my caffeine intake – how many cups of coffee I drank a day (five); how many Diet Cokes (three). She asked me what time I went to bed (10 p.m.) and what time I put my phone away (midnight). She asked how much alcohol I drank in a week (a bottle of wine … mostly on a Friday night) and what exercise I took (does getting public transport count?). She took note of how long I spent in front of my computer screen (eleven hours a day) and what I did in my leisure time (dating is a legitimate hobby, right?).

As we took this inventory, it became increasingly clear to me that a psychology degree was not necessary to solve at least part of my problem. The way I was living – well, I wouldn't treat a dog that way. Quite the opposite. If I saw a dog owner do this I would be ranting about the rightness of owning animals when it's clear you can't take care of them. Yet in that we all have bodies, we all own our own animal – and we frequently abuse it.

A teacher at the organization where I trained to be a coach once asked me a question that really made me wake up to this. We were talking about how hard I worked and how tired I was and I was just refusing to slow down. Then she asked me: 'Do you really want to be here? On this planet?'

It made me realize my body was more than just a fleshy

structure for carting my head around; that my physical self had needs and desires. If I wanted to be on this planet, I needed to stop ignoring the messages my body was giving me.

Every creature has different needs and preferences, and the first step is getting to know what our body likes and dislikes. When it comes to your own body, I'm a big believer that though it's good to also listen to experts, deep down you know your body best. That became especially obvious to me when I got ill.

I had chronic fatigue syndrome, or ME, for the best part of ten years, beginning at age thirteen. Doctors don't really understand what causes this illness, which along with extreme tiredness comes with delectable symptoms such as fierce muscle-pain, sore throats, dizziness and headaches. They also aren't sure what makes some people recover either. The severity of the symptoms changes from day to day, but in my case, at my worst I couldn't walk. My body felt so heavy and I felt so weak that I could only crawl to the toilet. Things got worse before they got better. It wasn't clear I would ever recover. It was rotten.

> The atoms that make up our body are mostly empty space. If we lost all our empty atomic space we would fit into a cube less than 1/500th of a centimetre on each side.[5]

I did learn a few things, though. Such as that there's nothing like having a 'mysterious' illness if you want a thousand contradictory pieces of advice propelled your way. Some people suggested I should sleep more; some said I was probably sleeping too much. Other people told me I should exercise (but … I can't walk!); meanwhile, some suggested total bed rest. Or that total bed rest wasn't enough and that I must completely rest my mind and not look or listen to a single thing. That I should change what I'm eating, that I should quit sugar, or dairy, or wheat, or only eat raw food. I should take this tonic twice daily, or drink Chinese herbal tea. That I had an allergy to electricity, or wool, or water. That I needed antidepressants.

And then if I did that and none of those things worked, I was definitely faking it. Sometimes I felt like actually being ill was only half the problem – the other half was managing people's reactions to it.

In the end, I made a slow recovery just continually doing what felt possible and fun. My granny moved in to look after me; we both wanted to move slowly but still find enjoyment in the little things, like a short walk and an ice cream by the canal. It took me a long while from that point to getting back to school and then it was a struggle from there to not beat myself up over all the things I could no longer do. I still get flare-ups from time to time.

I'm not a doctor, and I'm not telling you what to do. What I might suggest is that you check in with yourself, and see if your creature is happy with what you are doing now. Reflect on this without shame or judgement. Swap any 'shoulds' for 'coulds'. When we say we 'should' do something, it feels tight and punishing. Saying 'could' instead opens us up to possibility. Try it.

Once you find what feels good for you, think about making those choices a practice. Mark the space in your diary to exercise, rest, cuddle or get outside as 'sacred time' – non-negotiable slots in your day or week that you use to nourish yourself.

Commit to doing these 'sacred time' things regularly, even when your mind is tempted to resist or it becomes inconvenient, as a way of attending to your creature self.

This is a process. Calling it a practice signals to yourself that it is not a quick hit and it's okay if you don't get it right straight away. We are relearning how to love our creature selves. It doesn't happen overnight.

It's worth continuing to practise because we learn new ways of thinking and behaving through repetition. Choice plus action, over and over again, is the way we make lasting change in our lives.

Give yourself a score out of ten at the end of each section about how satisfied you are with this particular area of your life – this will give you clarity on where you might want to focus your attention first.

MOVEMENT

You can tell me you don't enjoy exercise, but don't tell me you don't enjoy movement. You *are* movement. Every cell of your body engages in activity every second of the day. We are all constantly in motion; it's the essence of who we are. When we stop moving, we die.

Movement is how we engage with the world; it's bodily expression. Physicality is one of the cornerstones of living.

This epiphany finally saw me embrace exercise.

That's right – being barked at by a sports teacher at the bottom of a gym rope didn't work and being told I wasn't 'beach-body ready' just made me feel angry. Gyms were smelly, noisy vanity-closets and team sports were just another way of feeling left out.

I bypassed the emotional landmine that is the exercise industry and instead viewed movement as my birthright as the owner of a body. To bastardize an oft-attributed Socrates quote, I told myself I would not grow old without seeing the beauty and strength of which my body was capable. It's not always easy, especially if you have a physical disability, but part of being human is working with what we have, day after day, to reach the most that is available to us.

It isn't about being 'good' at netball, or the best at tennis; it is just about enjoying how your body moves, in any way that feels good.

And *voila*! Exercise became fun. I rediscovered the joy that lay latent in my body when I started to make time for moving as expression rather than another obligation to fail at.

I dance, and I love the way no limb is left behind as you tell emotional stories with your body. The mental challenge of learning new moves means there is no space for anything but focus and joy.

I practise yoga every day. I like its goalless nature – every stretch is valued for its own unique place in your journey. I love that I keep discovering new muscles – and that my body begins to lengthen – and change shape, just as I breathe and relax into a position.

Exercise that gets my heart rate up has been an important part of strengthening my creature, too. When I first started coaching, I was working from home, and while I loved helping people, my body and mind felt heavy from the depth of the emotional service required daily. Yoga wasn't enough – I needed something faster to metabolize all those feelings running through me. That's the beauty of movement; if emotions are energetic information, then for me, moving quickly is energetic processing of that download.

Although I didn't begin consciously exercising as a way to challenge myself, it's something I've begun to lean into. A kind of alchemy happens in the mind when you practise strength and capability exercises. You might be training to make your legs stronger, but somehow you personally feel stronger, too. More powerful in your mind, stronger as a human, more capable to handle the curveballs that life throws at you. As I face the challenge of running that last mile against the wind and continually survive, I'm encouraged to take on challenges off the track, too. It probably helps that when I run I think of myself as Wonder Woman, in training to be a superhero.

Getting started

Even aspiring superheroes struggle to get out of bed sometimes. Fortunately, your body is incredibly adaptive and gets better at whatever you choose to do with it. Unfortunately, I had been training my body to sit down for eleven hours a day for the past decade. I didn't even think about beginning to exercise until the pain started.

After holding myself tightly at my desk for one day too many, my shoulders began screaming when I turned too fast, my neck seared with heat, I swear I could hear my wrists squeaking. I couldn't type on my phone for too long without feeling like my hand had morphed into painful concrete. I'd got so good at being sedentary, my body was seizing up.

Knowing I needed to move, though, still wasn't enough for me to actually begin exercising. It was about clearing the blocks that were stopping me from doing it, as well as giving myself some short-term carrots to get over that initial hurdle.

If you're struggling to move more, I hope by sharing what stopped me and how I got over that will give you some ideas.

'I don't have time'

First of all, is this really true? Because I actually did have time, but my mind threw this up as a real reason, when it was just an excuse. I was also trying to justify why I hadn't done it before, because I was a bit ashamed.

How I got over this: I hate gyms so I bought new running shoes and a backpack and kept them at work so I could jog at lunchtime or part of the way home. In this way, I actually felt like I was being extra productive, by commuting and exercising in one go – or using my break well: it wasn't like I had to 'manufacture' an extra slot in the day.

'I can't be bothered'

It can be hard to find the motivation. It can feel tedious. I know, it's how I felt, too.

How I got over this: I told myself 'Just do it for fifteen minutes – you can stop at any time after that'. Turns out that after fifteen minutes I began to enjoy it. There are loads of fifteen-minute exercise classes on YouTube, too.

The other thing that helped is getting people to hold me (somewhat) accountable – finding people who wanted to do thirty-day challenges with me on YouTube. There's a January thirty-day yoga challenge with a new video every day and I wanted to do all of them to catch up. See if you can set yourself a challenge and find yourself an accountability buddy.

'It's boring'

It *was* boring. I was used to the speed of breaking-news headlines, my thoughts moving extra fast on adrenaline. In comparison, my body felt slow and heavy and clunky, and frankly, I felt no good at it.

How I got over this: instead of going for coffee I would go for a class or a walk with someone. I told myself that my response to the thought of exercise here was just showing me the state of my mind – it's so busy it can't switch off to work at a different speed. I used reverse psychology, saying to myself that the less I was enjoying this, the more I really needed this. I also looked for things I *did* find fun – like dancing.

'I'm too tired. I should rest'

Here's where you need a bit of love to soothe your reluctance. Whenever I felt like this I would treat myself – and not with food. I'd use these treats as actions; as kind, pleasurable rituals to ease myself into whatever I was resisting. For yoga I would first draw the curtains and light lots of candles. I bought a new 'exercise' perfume to pep me up for the gym and shift my mental space. For dance, I'd allow myself to spend money on a class – or I'd buy new socks for running. I'd remind myself that it was my mind that was tired, or overstimulated, not my body.

'I feel fat'

Yes, every time I chose to exercise I had to face my body. Or rather, I had to face my feelings about my body. (This was when I realized I not only had shame over my weight, but I had shame over feeling less than body positive, too. Ah, judging my own judgement, the shame about shame. My favourite style of self-indulgence.)

My tired, thick body made me feel as though moving it was pointless – that I'd never lose weight or get fit. I'd get this heavy feeling in my stomach, which felt like it was telling me, 'Why bother?'

How I got over this: no magic button for this one. The more I sat with these feelings and thoughts, the more I got used to them, and the less uncomfortable they became – a bit like exercise. I reminded myself that choosing to move was in itself an act of self-care, which made moving less about weight loss and more about the experience itself – and I focused on how I could do this gracefully, training myself to trust that moving was good for me. I thanked my body that it could move, for holding me up, or giving me endorphins.

How could you solve this problem? Get creative – and loosen the purse strings a little if you can afford it. What do you spend on things that don't benefit your body?

If, like me, you don't think the excuses your brain is giving you are the real reason you're resisting exercise, get a friend you trust to help you. All they need to do is ask the following questions and thank you for each answer you give:

1. *'What's stopping you from exercising?'*
2. *'What's underneath that?'*
3. *'What are you resisting?'*

Let them repeatedly ask until they feel they have a true answer – maybe set a timer for five or ten minutes. Then, when you have a list of about five or more things, brainstorm with them to give you other ideas for getting over this hump.

REST

It's nearly four hundred years since Isaac Newton said, 'What goes up, must come down' and almost definitely didn't get hit on the head by an apple.

It's fun to be feeling up and active, and sometimes it does feel like we have a lot to do, but we all need to come down. The trick, I've learnt, is to plan rest periods, because quite often we aren't so good at taking rest, even when it's needed. How familiar do phrases like this sound? 'I won't take a lunch-break – I don't have the time', or 'Yoga makes me sleepy … it's too boring.' Another one I sometimes hear is: 'I won't sit down or I'll never get up again.'

Hey! Slowing down only feels uncomfortable when we're going way too fast. Yoga isn't making you sleepy; you're goddamn exhausted! And sit down, or your body will force you to sit down. Everything can wait while you take a break and live. Promise. The truth is that the more jarring it feels to slow down, the greater the difference between stillness and the pace you were going, and the more your body and mind needs to pause.

I like this story about Mahatma Gandhi, who when told by his advisors that he had a busy day ahead and might need to skip his morning meditation, said instead that because of that he must actually meditate for two hours instead of one. For twice as much work, twice as much space and clarity is needed.

We think we go fast because we have so much to do and it's the only way to get it all done. That's nonsense. Slow your mind down, slow your body down, and the things you don't need to worry about will drop away of their own accord. Our vision clears when we slow down – we can't see what's necessary when we're running at high speed. On top of that we can then actually attend to the things that are important with the attention they deserve. That includes the people we care about, whose feelings get trampled on when we are flying by the seat of our pants from one frenetic activity to another. Going too fast makes us impatient and irritable with the ones we love, and in turn we can either internalize that frustration with ourselves for not being compassionate or seek to further disconnect from anyone or anything that might get in our way, which leads to isolation. It's not an honourable way to live, but we all find ourselves there at times. I use my irritability as the canary in the coal mine; the more it flares up, the more I know I need to slow things down.

We aren't used to this. People mistake speed for efficiency, confuse stress with self-importance and substitute busyness for meaning.

Too many of us live our lives at manufactured speed, everything whizzing past us at a hundred miles an hour. Fuelled by adrenaline, we can hardly see what's going on around us accurately, let alone feel or make decisions well. On one level we know we are going too fast. We layer sensation on top of sensation, activity over activity, sugar on top of caffeine. Anything to avoid feeling the deep fatigue, the tension, the sadness that's building up in our bodies. Then our scheduled holiday arrives and we get a horrific cold, or we take a few deep breaths and burst into tears.

Unwind well

We all get busy and up in our heads; but we don't need to stay there. It's much better to unwind a little bit at a time and naturally – to come down from busyness deliberately, rather than wait until your body crashes out and bed rest is inconveniently forced upon you.

The question you want to ask yourself is 'How do I like to relax?' If you don't know, get curious. Active ways of resting might be things like reading a book, going for a walk, taking a yoga class, ringing your grandma – even cleaning or cooking. See if you can think of five right now. Passive ones might be having a salt bath, a cuddle, a massage. Maybe watching a Disney movie. Experiment with what feels good.

Change the way you think about rest – not as inactivity but rather as developing the skill of slowing down. Sports coaches schedule strict rest days for their athletes; it's a vital part of their training. You want to be able to change gears – not have only one speed you can operate at.

It's hard to prioritize rest, because modern society doesn't seem to value relaxation. But even fields have fallow years – in which, deliberately, nothing is planted – to give the soil a chance to revitalize itself.

This is ancient wisdom. Contrary to popular thought, rest

is how you grow stronger. It's regeneration. Every culture has a rest day – it's been like that since time began.

The most loving thing you can do for yourself, at any moment, is slow. it. right. down. Stop. Take a deep breath. Soften your jaw. Allow your belly to expand. Let your shoulders sink down. Allow the skin on your face to release. This is a pace that is more caring for you, for your body and for whatever it is you are attending to. Look how much easier it is to feel and see life when you're in this softer spot.

> Parkinson's law is the adage that work expands to fill the time available to complete it. This law was invented by a civil servant in the 1950s, who had observed it in practice during his time working in government.[6]

Sometimes, people come to me for coaching, and they say, 'I need help managing my time.' They turn up for their sessions every week, and they seem to have accomplished a lot in their lives. They really don't have a time-management problem; they have an 'overwhelm' problem, they have a self-love problem and they have a trust problem. I empathize. I think I was going so fast at one point in my life that I could have made being a meditation teacher stressful. Sometimes the thoughts were popping so fast in my head that I could barely get the words out.

So I understand when I hear clients say, 'Basically, I need

three of me.' I tell them, 'Oh yes, and what if I gave you three of you? You'd be back here next week, saying I think I actually need six of me.' The problem is never that there's not enough of you; it's that you think you are not enough, and one symptom of that pain is that you're trying to do too much.

When you slow down, regardless of the number of things you have to do, you tell yourself, 'I want to enjoy life,' That life is important and you are important. If you only had one slice of a delicious dessert, you would savour it, taking each bite slowly and deliberately and with relish. Why wouldn't you do the same with life? Cramming your life with piles of nonsense just makes it feel shorter.

Good things feel better stretched out. Feelings can breathe given airtime. Time dilutes pain, too. Everyone wins when we slow. it. right. down. With space, the unimportant drops off, inviting in clarity and creating more room. And more often than not, it's love that rushes into those gaps, something we could all do with more of.

Try making it your mission to schedule half an hour of nothing in your diary every day. Put it in before everything else.

DRINKING, SMOKING, DRUGS

First things first, and this might be a shocker, but whatever you are doing, it's okay. If you're drinking too much, smoking too much, or taking too many drugs, that's okay. It might not be healthy, it might not even be legal, but I'm not a doctor, police officer or judge, and from where I'm sitting, in my human skin, with my human mind, you're not a *bad* person.

That's not quite all I have to say on the issue though, because let's face it, smoking is a terrible ROI ('Yes, I will pay money to endure a slow death and smell pungently'). Meanwhile, alcohol is attractively packaged poison and illegal drugs are a brilliant shortcut to having a whole host of totally chaotic situations and people show up in your life.

So why say it's okay? Well, I heartily approve of whatever situation you find yourself in with drink, drugs or smoking because you're here now, and shaming or admonishing you won't solve anything. You already know all the things about why you shouldn't do it. And guess what? You do them anyway. So let's not go down that particular cul-de-sac of schoolteacher righteousness. I do and have done some of the bad things, too. Telling myself off (or someone else telling me off) just makes me feel stressed out, which in turn makes me want to seek the crutch I was being told off about in the first place.

The thing is, if you're using substances, smoking or drinking, you probably have really legitimate reasons for doing the things you're doing. I'm guessing it's more than just 'this feels temporarily good', too. You might be smoking because you enjoy the connection, or the break you get outside. You might be drinking because you find it difficult to relax.

You might have some feelings that you're not quite sure how to work with. Maybe the people you're hanging out with have that problem, and you're just going along with it because you want to feel part of something. It could be that there are situations you feel particularly uncomfortable in and you don't know how to manage that. It could be that life just feels a bit sucky and why not check out and care about nothing for a while.

This might not be a full-blown addiction, where it's about to take over your life, but it's still an unhealthy way to relate to your emotions: even if it's 'letting off steam' with six beers on a Friday.

Think about whether you want to continue down that path. Because it might be fun occasionally, but it's not the best use of body, mind, time or money. Plus, you might have been drinking, smoking or taking drugs to help you avoid or 'numb' a particular issue or feeling, and unless everything has magically changed, including your thinking, well, you're just going to need more and more to help you cope. It doesn't really solve the issue; it's just a stop gap. The drinking, smoking or drugs is just papering over the top. A sticking plaster for a broken shoulder. There's only so long it will work for you. If indeed, it works well at all.

Addiction

More frustrating than all of that, at least for me, is that these substances, which you may have used originally to let go and feel more free, actually end up putting more constraints on you.

Your choices get hijacked by a bunch of toxins because, biologically and psychologically, it becomes harder and harder to turn them down. The reason you first said yes to the wine, the cigarette, or the line, is not the reason you are going to keep saying yes. And at some point the reason you say yes will end up being because you don't feel you can say no.

You can.

It's just hard.

The reasons we do these things is complicated and we even hide them from ourselves. We didn't want to confront them in the first place, which is why we started drinking/ smoking/taking drugs. Unfortunately, the original issue will not magically disappear once you stop doing the thing either. You'll still need a way to handle the whatever-was-troubling-you in the first place.

There's always a reason you are doing what you are doing, or started doing what you are doing, and it's worth investigating this, ideally with a therapist. Then, when you find out what the unhealthy activity gives you, you can find out a way to replicate that without the substance.

Perhaps you'll find that if you're a little less punishing with yourself, you don't need to drink as much. Or if you schedule something with a sober friend, they can help you keep on track during a time when you know you like to drink (maybe after a stressful day). Find an activity you like, that relaxes you or is fun, or that even gives you a high; that is healthy and doesn't involve the substance. It might involve making some new friends.

This is not medical advice and neither am I an addiction expert. I heartily endorse enrolling on a twelve-step programme if any of these substances have appeared or are appearing in your life in a way that feels hard to handle. Notice I don't limit this to whether or not you're the individual actually doing the consuming – because that's the thing about these substances: they have a large radius of influence.

Although the biggest twelve-step programme is Alcoholics Anonymous, there are also a number of less well-known groups that follow this pattern for countering addiction – for example, Clutterers Anonymous, Underearners Anonymous, and OLGA – On-line Gamers Anonymous.

Additionally, if you have an addiction and want help, get some medical advice, because there's a wealth of knowledge and support out there for how to quit effectively. Many people have walked this path before you, so you will be well-held.

I have the utmost empathy for anyone who's struggled with addiction or substance misuse, or even if you're just someone who knows they like a certain thing a bit too much. I have addiction issues in my family, have had my own personal battles, and have met a lot of recovering addicts. This latter group are some of the strongest, most courageous sensitive people I know.

Using substances, even recreationally, is just a manifestation of something happening persistently inside us that wants and deserves our attention and that we're very uncomfortable with; we don't want to look at it and see what it might need. Sometimes, it's just something that needs to be felt, an emotion that needs to be released or expressed and we don't know how to let it out – it doesn't feel socially acceptable. It might even feel unsafe. And so we seek to numb it or bury it.

We are all coping with such things. People who 'use' aren't any different from the person who is excessive in their gym attendance, or the compulsive shopper, or the workaholic. Even the person who is just incredibly busy in life – busy avoiding their own feelings. We all try to avoid, repress and numb; it's just that our methods often look different – some are healthier than others – and some are deemed less shameful.

If you take one thing away from this section it's that I don't think there is anything to be ashamed about in addiction. Drugs, smoking and drinking are not good for our bodies, though. Let's try and be a little kinder with ourselves and choose the loving thing.

Try to keep a diary of how much you drink/smoke/consume, and notice when this happens. What thoughts are going through your head when you go for them? What feelings do you have?

SKIN TIME

We have a deep primitive need for physical touch – an aching appetite that has become so taboo in our society that we all but pretend it doesn't exist. This isn't by any means necessarily a desire for sexual contact, though, for some, sex is the only acceptable way to get that need met.

Psychologists call it 'skin hunger'. Prisoners kept in solitary confinement know this peculiar starvation well. Chelsea Manning, who spent nine months isolated in this way, called it 'no touch torture'.[7]

Convicted murderer Peter Collins, who died of cancer in a Canadian prison, made a film called *Fly in the Ointment* about a prolonged period in solitary confinement. In it, he describes how he was so hungry for physical contact that a fly that landed on his leg excited him, and he imagined it was the touch of his wife.

'I was greedy for human touch so I closed my eyes and pretended it was her fingers,' he explains.

That experience nourished him so much that during his time in solitary confinement, he would bite the inside of his cheek and smear the blood on his leg to attract more flies.

This is an extreme example but, increasingly, many of us are living such isolated lives that lack of physical contact – or 'skin time' as I like to call it, affects more than just prisoners. Human touch just doesn't happen as naturally as it should any more. We are all living further apart. One woman who follows me on Twitter, but didn't want to be named, told me:

'My good friends are all people I met through social media and we talk daily but it's not the same. My best friend has moved away and I'm in a long-distance relationship.'

The concept of community (more on this later) as it once was is crumbling, leaving older people and those without partners or families at risk of loneliness. A friend who works as a GP told me that she suspects a few elderly patients regularly come in for an examination when nothing is wrong, purely for the physical contact.

The increasingly vivid issues of sexual consent and harassment mean platonic touch, especially across genders, is a sensitive issue. When I asked across my social-media networks, one man told me he deeply missed physical contact when not in a relationship, but was scared to ask for a hug 'in case it was taken the wrong way'. He added, 'I've not had anyone initiate it with me either.'

In some friendship groups it is not usual to hug, particularly man-to-man. One of the people in my meditation group told me that her friends hug so lightly that it just feels like a pat on the back. When she got some cats, something strange happened: 'Suddenly I had this affectionate response to being touched that was so deeply nourishing. It's why changing my living circumstances and possibly moving away from my cats is a hard no.'

Meanwhile, in some circles touch is still considered 'creepy' or 'effeminate', leaving some men afraid to ask for this primal human need to be met for fear of being mocked or excluded.

'I'd be scared of looking gay,' one man told me.

Another said he'd love to but, 'I don't know how to. No one taught me. I never saw it modelled. None of my male friends did either, with rare exceptions. I'm afraid of it. Of the reaction, rejection, discomfort. I remember vividly travelling in Turkey – male platonic touch is just normal there. I was shocked. Jealous.'

Touch as therapy

I was a pupil at a boarding school, and when I arrived there I volunteered to teach people with special needs how to use computers. One man who had impaired brain and motor function put his hand on my knee and didn't remove it. I realized it was the first time I'd been touched in about four weeks, as I was a bit shy with friends and I hadn't been home. It made me feel really sad.

There are still times now where I forget how much I love and need comforting, platonic touch. I was really upset once and a friend hugged me and stroked my hair and it just felt blissfully soothing. Another time, I was sitting in my front room with a male friend having an unusually honest conversation, when he said to me, 'I'd really like to give you a cuddle. Can I?' I'd been running this headache that hadn't shifted all day, and as I put my head on his chest, this embarrassingly large exhale came from me and the pain in my head just shifted. Skin hunger always creeps up on me slowly, the need I don't realize I have until it gets satiated and then my whole body relaxes and sighs with contentment.

Touch is the first sense to develop, appearing at eight weeks after conception.

On a chemical level, supportive touch triggers hormonal changes equivalent to knocking back a well-being cocktail. Even just a hug lowers levels of cortisol, the stress hormone, while at the same time increasing the release of oxytocin, also known as the 'love' or 'trust' hormone.

Specifically, oxytocin has been found to increase self-esteem, optimism, generosity, build trust and foster bonding. Studies show that a rise in oxytocin can also relieve pain (ah – that's where my headache went!) and has anti-inflammatory properties, too.

When we receive or give touch the same areas of the brain light up as those that are activated when we smell something we like, or taste sweet things. Hugs reward the brain in the same way as a piece of chocolate might.

Finding touch

If you're not in a relationship, don't have family close by or your friends aren't the hugging sort, getting the physical touch you need can be difficult. Maybe you do have some close contact, the odd dry handshake and quick hug, but it's not enough, and you feel vulnerable and awkward asking for the type of gentle touch you crave. (**Note:** that's important – *ask*, don't take.)

Well, first know that you aren't alone in experiencing this skin-loneliness. I received dozens of messages just from people in my own social network when I asked if anyone felt deprived of touch. A quick google and you'll see multiple posts in forums asking for advice on how to seek this platonic touch without entering into a relationship. There are dozens of cuddle parties arranged every year in London, where I live, as more and more people meet up to mutually exchange physical affection in a way that sadly just isn't a usual part of daily life. It's why some individuals work as 'professional cuddlers', offering therapeutic touch in exchange for fifty pounds an hour.

If this isn't for you, there are other ways to get the healing touch you need – visiting a body worker or a masseuse. You could join a partner-based dancing class or get a pet. In the meantime, just lovingly rubbing in moisturizer after a bath in a way that feels luxurious to the skin, also feels like a tactile treat. Simple activities like a bath can be transformed just through the beauty of intention, and through deliberately feeling your skin, the soap suds, the heat of the water, and how your body relaxes under your own touch. Place a hand on your belly and one on your heart and sink into the hot water and relax.

See if you can summon up the courage to offer a hug when the moment next feels right. You might get a no, but on the up side, it might make someone's day. I was outside Charing Cross station once when a homeless man came up to me asking for change. I had no cash on me, but he looked pretty dejected, so I asked if he wanted a hug. He nodded and I gave him a hug. When I pulled away he was crying. I think my heart broke a little bit that day.

FOOD

I have one over-arching philosophy that applies to both food and sex: whatever you choose to put or not put in your mouth has no impact whatsoever on your value as a human being. Let me say it even clearer: the scales are not a scorecard. Your weight is not your worth.

Taking that as read, most of us could choose to eat in a way that nourishes both mind and body more. We know the benefits of healthy eating. So why is it so hard to do? Well, it's complicated.

Food is fuel, yes, but it's also a sensory pleasure, a cultural signifier, a social activity and a way to bond. It can be a creative outlet, a coping mechanism, a source of guilt, a mission or a moral code.

On top of that exhausting melee, from the moment we're born we're bombarded with contradictory conscious and subconscious messages on how to feel about food.

By the time you reach your eighteenth birthday, you will have had 33,000 learning experiences with food (based on three meals and a couple of snacks a day).

That's one hell of a relationship history to unravel.

Learning how to behave around food differently, if that

is what you want or need to do to help your body, is not something that happens overnight. But it is doable. I know because I've been there. I've got eating disorders in my family and have had disordered eating myself – I've put on 30 kg and lost it – and gained it and lost it. My eating feels good sometimes, and other times, I slip back into old patterns.

Often, when we're really focused or excited, we will forget to eat at all. Sometimes, I'm so buzzed or absorbed by what I'm doing that I stop checking in with the body that allows me to do those things. I don't want to lose the flow of how I'm feeling, so I grip on tight to whatever emotional high I'm riding and then crash out later. It's not a caring thing to do for my body.

We can be emotional eaters, too. I use pizza as a solution when hunger isn't the problem. So I'll eat when I'm sad or lonely: hot mushrooms and cheese as a substitute for a loving hug and a shoulder to cry on.

Sometimes we eat because we're tired or stressed. Chocolate chip cookies aren't known for their ability to make reading about Brexit less complicated, or for solving an argument with your sister, but hey, I use them like that.

Biologically, it sort of makes sense that many of us might eat like this. When we eat food, dopamine – a feel-good neurotransmitter, or chemical in the brain – gets released. This activates the reward and pleasure centres in the brain. Certain foods give us a particularly sharp spike in dopamine, including high fat and sugar foods.

Then, over time, we come to associate feeling good

with certain foods. We reach for a chocolate bar every time something stressful happens and we start to feel anxious. Biology prompts behaviour that becomes a habit. At that point, we just start to coast away on circular autopilot, eating how we've always eaten because we've always eaten that way.

This is a very potted version of the relationship between food, body and mind in an area that is crowded with rapidly expanding research. The best I can do is explain how I changed my own eating to serve me better.

Befriend your food

This is about adjusting your relationship to food; just as you would do in a relationship with a person, it makes sense to get to know your food too. There's a *lot* of information out there and not all of it is helpful.

At the end of the day, for me, it's just been about getting savvy with basic nutritional information and finding out what I'm eating, and why certain foods might make me feel good or bad, happy or grumpy. Taking an interest and making informed choices.

It means knowing that certain fruits contain more sugar than others – mango is a fruit with lots of sugar in, and so are grapes. Strawberries and blueberries less so. In general, the more tropical a fruit is, or the hotter the climate it grows in, the more sugar it is likely to contain.

It means accepting that added sugar is added sugar and therefore means calories, no matter what form that sugar takes. Fruit juice is full of sugar, even if it's just juiced fruit.

Sweet, natural foods like honey can have some additional health benefits, such as antibacterial properties. At the end of the day, it is still sugar, though – and there's plenty of research that shows too much sugar is not good for our bodies.

Sugar is one type of carbohydrate. Starch is another. Carbohydrates provide the body with energy.

Some vegetables have more carbs in (green, leafy vegetables have fewer carbs; root vegetables – the ones that grow underground – have more carbs).

There's a difference, however, between carbs in vegetables and 'refined carbs' in bread and sweets. Refined-carb foods cause a spike in energy levels, which initially feels great, until you crash and want more – starting a craving cycle.

Refined carbs have had the fibre stripped out; they've been processed, which is not great, as fibre is good for the gut; it helps clean it out. Things like oats have lots of fibre in them – soluble fibre that turns into a gel in the gut and can prevent fat from being absorbed, and slows down digestion, which can stop energy spikes. There's also insoluble fibre, which can't be digested at all, but speeds up the movement and processing of waste. Foods high in insoluble fibre include kidney beans, popcorn and wheat bran. Fibre is also thought to make you feel full; it can be found in nuts, too – another nutritious food. They are high calorie, though.

Knowing what are high-calorie foods or the opposite can help guide your eating, if you're watching your energy intake.

Five valuable tips for eating well:

1. *Plan: if there are times you're tempted by convenience food or takeaways, get stuff in that's easy to eat and that you like, so you have a nice option for yourself, too.*

2. *Don't cut off your legs because you fell over once. So you had some food that wasn't so healthy. That's okay! You don't have to give up and eat all the pizza in the world now.*

3. *Have some high-quality distractions − if you eat when you're bored, make sure you have other things to do that are just as tempting.*

4. *Drink more water. Buy a flask and keep it with you at all times.*

5. *Carry good snacks around with you (such as a banana, or a small bag of nuts or seeds).*

Knowing what foods contain certain vitamins and minerals and what those vitamins and minerals do for the body can be useful, too. For example, spinach and apricots (even some dark chocolate) contain iron − which importantly contributes to the healthy oxygen in red blood cells.

Food can affect mood. Spinach is also thought to be good for anxiety as it contains a lot of magnesium. Some refer to the gut as the 'second brain' − there are more than one hundred-million neurons lining our enteric nervous system, which stretches from our oesophagus to our anus and is nine metres long. That's more neurons, or nerve cells, than are in our spinal cord; it's thought that we have that many so that the brain doesn't have to get too involved with the complicated process of the digestion – the gut has a basic knowledge of what to do itself.

We know that our moods affect our stomach (think how when we're excited we feel butterflies, when we're nervous we might feel sick, or when we're very anxious we may need to go to the toilet), but we're only just beginning to tap the surface of how our gut bacteria affects our mood. For example, one small study[8] showed that women who ate a bacteria-containing yoghurt for a month had changes in parts of the brain that processes emotion, suggesting a decrease in anxiety.

Oranges are also thought to be a great mood booster because of the high amounts of B^{12} as well as vitamin C, (though red peppers have more vitamin C in them than oranges). Part of getting friendly with your food might mean knowing that fruits and vegetables that are orange and yellow have beta-carotene in them (think carrots) and the body can turn this into vitamin A – which among other things is good for eye health.

I now know that certain oils are awesome for my brain, which loves fatty acids such as omega-3 and -6, and that this oil comes in fish and nuts.

Supermarket shopping

Befriending my food meant I started getting curious about what was in my food and where it came from. I began being that person reading the backs of the packets in the supermarket. Then I started not being very impressed with the copious list of unintelligible ingredients in ready meals. I started wanting to cook more rather than eat things that were mass produced. I realized fat free doesn't mean fewer calories and that less calories doesn't mean fewer carbs.

I struggle to eat a lot of meat now after a particularly gruesome discovery I made as a journalist into exactly how abattoirs operated. Reading more on how factory farming works, it sat so sickly in my stomach, well, I don't really want a chlorinated chicken sandwich anytime soon. I only eat meat from farms that are approved by animal welfare charities.

Sure, sometimes I get lazy and go pick up something quick and tasteless from the supermarket that can be heated up in five minutes. But now I know what's in that food, it makes it all the harder to skip out on choosing what's best for my body. Choosing the packaged meal feels like a less caring thing to do for myself because I'm aware of what's nourishing. Finding out the benefits of what I ate encouraged me to make loving decisions about what I put in my mouth.

Know how it feels

Once you've got to know a little bit about how food works in theory, it's good to tune into the experience of eating that food, and discovering your preferences.

Start with how it feels in your mouth. The rubbery, slimy, fibrous sensation that accompanies masticating a banana – the slightly sticky after-texture that it leaves in your mouth. The cleansing, acidic taste of lemon, which can sting your palette into semi-numbness. A dense yet crumbly cheese. The injection of sweet juice that squirts across your palette as you burst a grape between your teeth.

I started to chew and digest mindfully, rather than chomping manically. Could I relish every mouthful? What would happen if I slowed down while I consumed?

I made sure I ate sitting down, without reading or watching TV, but just have eating be what it was. I started to notice what the sensation of being satisfied felt like in my body.

I checked in with myself to see which foods not only tasted delicious while I was eating them, but also felt good in my body afterwards. How mashed potato gave me this warm heavy feeling, how eggs got me energized but stable. How tomatoes made me feel … horny.

I also noticed it actually feels better if I don't eat certain foods – even if my creature pretends it's craving it. Sugar is my nemesis, my gateway drug to neglectful eating. One brownie and I just can't stop. I'll have dessert in restaurants but otherwise I won't keep sugar in the house. For me, it's addictive. Every time I have it, it takes another week for the cravings to wear off again, to stop being irritable and restless because I'm not having cake for breakfast.

One thing I noticed as I gathered facts about food and tuned into the feelings was that I seemed to have an awful lot of ideas around food that were more than just science and sensation. My larder was fully stocked with stories, too.

Unravelling your food fairy tales

See if you can catch yourself telling yourself stories about food. Are potatoes the enemy? Is cake a rebellious treat and fruit a boring obligation?

When I'm loading my plate with meaning as well as complex carbohydrates, it affects not only my choices, but also how I enjoy my food and sometimes even how I feel about myself.

So I began to deconstruct the narrative, and either challenge it or change it for one that served me better.

I wanted food to feel less like a guilty pleasure and more like what it was: nutrition. If you want to do this, ask yourself if you can make foods that nourish you feel like a treat. Give your food a good story, an attractive one. For me I repackaged blueberries as a superfood in my head, looked up all their nutritional benefits, remembered they were expensive – therefore valuable – and said 'yes' to all of these things with every mouthful. Unsurprisingly, they tasted a lot better.

Tell yourself any story that works for you

What I will say is: make sure your story is positive. There are three reasons for that:

1. *There are already too many unhappy stories in this world. Trust me, I'm a journalist. Let's not add to them with ones we've created deliberately to punish ourselves. No one needs more negative stories in their brains.*
2. *Our nervous system has two responses to help us live safe*

and happy lives. One is the sympathetic nervous system – the 'fight or flight' response. The other is the parasympathetic nervous system – this allows us to relax and feel calm. If the sympathetic nervous system is activated, the body cannot digest food – after all, if you're being chased by a bear, it's not really of immediate importance to metabolize; much better shift the energy to arms and legs, so you can make your life-or-death decisions. The thing is, we can go into this primitive survival mode if we are stressed or even if we beat ourselves up through anxiety – and this then makes it much harder for us to digest the nutrients from our food. It also encourages our body to hoard fat. Much better then, if we are eating, to consider how delicious and wonderful the food is, than make ourselves feel guilty.

3. *Food is enjoyable. Eating can be an immense pleasure. I cannot see any purpose in any activity that denies, diminishes or demonizes our appetites. If you're eating for the joy of eating, in a way that respects your body, it's unlikely that you will overindulge. Distortions occur when, like I did, you use food as a focus to distract you from uncomfortable emotional states, or you eat so fast you don't feel full.*

Food matters. It affects how we feel and how we are fuelled physically. The nutrients we absorb can affect our mood and our mood can affect our digestion. Learning the basics about food, the scientific nuts and bolts of nutrition, alongside observing how we feel physically and emotionally when we eat a certain way, can help inform our diet. Every body is different, and eating what feels good for you might be different to what feels good for me. Essentially, food is this wonderful tool that can support your emotional and physical health and is also pleasurable. Woop!

Feed yourself. Nourish yourself. Enjoy yourself, with food.

NATURE

Getting outside and into nature is the most underrated activity that benefits your body and your mind – and your soul. And it's free, most of the time.

To be fair, its image has had a bit of a revamp recently, what with coverage of wellness treatments like 'forest bathing' (standing with trees to make you feel better) and eco-therapy (getting outside and doing something active), but we've still got a long way to go before we give the wealth and beauty of nature the same social importance as the culture and buzz of the city.

There's a tendency to associate urban centres with investment, progress and talent, and the countryside with isolation, retreat and stagnation. It's somewhat of a self-fulfilling prophecy in terms of the economics of it all.

Yet, money aside, this view fails to take into account the life-affirming, sense-awakening, mind-freshening nature of greenery.

If you give a f★★k about your mental health, about your

body, about how you stay alive, you have to care about nature. And not just in the abstract, buying sustainable produce and shopping for organic food, but by actually getting out there. Get outside and get some green (not that one). Connect with your wild side. It's where you came from and it's where you're going back to.

Perhaps that's why we're a little shy of the landscape. It reminds us that we're smaller than we sometimes like to think. That even the big man in his big job, in his big office, feeling smug at his big maple-wood desk is the same as any of us in the maple-wood forest.

That isn't something to fear. I think of being in these humbling landscapes as an outlook bomb: you know the ones – they go off in your brain sometimes, something clicks about what is really true and important and it totally explodes your perspective, shifting your outlook. There's a lot we can learn from nature about the way to live.

While walking in the countryside and observing the way trees and bushes grow to fill the space available, I realize nature doesn't question who it is, or what it is, whether it should or shouldn't be there, it just *is* and it expands to be the most it can possibly be in the space it's given. Seeing vines snake up a rock face, or branches that bend in the wind, I think about how we, too, could learn from their generosity in the face of adversity; they don't fight it, but flex with it. How we could seek to adapt to changes in our external circumstances, in the landscape of our own lives, with similar grace. Nature only seeks to keep growing, to keep being what it is to the best of its ability, developing around obstacles in its path, and making those impediments beautiful simply by its presence. It overcomes them simply by growing.

Nothing is 'wrong' in nature – it embraces everything. There is a part for everything in the ecosystem. Nothing ever dies; it simply changes form and returns back to the forest floor. With such abundance, perhaps that's why it doesn't wait to be asked to give to you, but nourishes your being as soon as you enter its soft, ferny fronds, without ever expecting anything in return. Replenishing is in its nature and it doesn't question whether that's fair or right, but just follows its instinct. I sometimes think that love is our essential nature too; we just get a bit distracted by all the fear and busyness and forget to be ourselves. Luckily, the option is always there to remember – just try and be moved by inspiration rather than by desperation, although desperation was how I found the joy in nature again.

Take off your shoes and socks

I'm not sure when I first realized I was so thirsty for nature – I think it was while I was doing the last six months of my news editing job and there was this horrible push-pull between wanting to do it and not just do it, but do it really well – all the while simultaneously knowing that it wasn't right for me. I spent that six months throwing myself at something that I was simultaneously repelled by. The headlines weren't making it any easier – excruciating misery and arguing politicians as usual. I felt drained.

I live and work in central London, and while it's not the heavy smog-filled beast of industrial Victoriana, it can be a little bald on the nature front if you don't go looking for it. I found myself wandering to the park every lunchtime, as if magnetically pulled by the trees and water away from the painful chaos of the news. Walking on the path with other people wasn't enough. I had to run into the wooded areas and actually feel myself surrounded. To stroke the leaves, touch the rough bark; to take my shoes and socks off and feel the grass beneath my feet. I realized I hadn't done this in months. My toes didn't know what the earth felt like.

We don't think of being outdoors in nature as something vital, and yet this word comes from the Latin 'vitalis', meaning 'of, or belonging to, life' – and what is more alive than nature? Those lunchtimes in the park where I covered my calves with crunchy leaves and spoke to squirrels, it was the only thing that saved me from the ugliness in the headlines poisoning my heart. The simplicity and connection in the wild order of nature, the power independent of human meddling, I found intensely restorative.

We know this intuitively, but studies show it, too. People living close to trees and green spaces are less likely to be obese, inactive or taking antidepressants.[9] Nature-based activities can also help people who are suffering from mental ill-health and can contribute to a reduction in levels of anxiety, stress and depression.[10] There's an increasing body of research into this area, as more and more of us come to realize that the soothing effects of being surrounded by beautiful landscapes is not a 'nice extra' but a necessity for our own well-being, and scientists seek to prove it.

The oldest living organism in the world is a tree – or trees. It's called Pando, or Trembling Giant, and is a colony of aspen trees spread over 106 acres. It's in Utah and its root system shows it's actually one individual organism that's 80,000 years old.

What I love about nature is when you're outside, you're never alone. Not really. Everything around you is instinctive, living, wilderness, and yet has a place and a purpose. It's bigger than you and yet you are part of it. It's hard not to be comforted by that when it feels like it's you against a world where everything is wrong and everyone is hurting. It draws from me a long exhale. I think the plants make us feel like this on purpose so they can get their CO_2. Their best interests are our best interests, too.

Try making it your mission to get to know all the green spaces in your area, so that you have a good idea of where to go if you start to feel burnt out. Develop favourites. Commit to spending twenty minutes in one, at least once a week. While there, take a look at the trees and grass and what's around you and see what lessons you can learn from the way nature adapts and grows in the environment. Touch the grass beneath you, or the bark of a tree for five seconds with the palm of your hand (even if you feel a little silly).

IMAGINATION

Consider the imagination as an unseen muscle for magic – the genitals of the brain, if you will. Like our reproductive organs, the imagination is the birthplace of creativity, with the same dark power of sexual energy. Too many of us abuse our incredible capacity for imagination, spending most of our lives throwing its might on the useless and the banal or constructing our own personal mental hell. We have imaginary arguments with our boss or our colleagues – or daydream about what's for dinner. While there's nothing wrong with expending your imagination on such pursuits, only exercising them like this is the equivalent of using a silk couture gown to clean your toilet.

Similarly, using your imagination solely for escapism is a little like junk food for your soul. Imagination lives at the border between reality and dreams – it's a flying machine that carries visions as its cargo, transporting fantasies from one realm into another. It's not meant to issue one-way tickets.

Imagination holds no prejudice or preference. It will carry light or dark across this veil – it will import genius or madness, with the power to infect or transform our worlds. Use it well.

It's clear there's something a little bit special about our imagination – the ability to conjure and connect concepts, pictures, symbols and movies that may not yet exist. This power just doesn't follow common-sense rules. Consider this:

- *Children are better at it than adults.*
- *It speeds up when we slow down – and is most productive when we are least productive, feeding off boredom, quietness and solitude.*
- *It is the most effective way we create change and is also the main thing responsible for holding us back.*
- *It constructs and destructs.*

Imagination is held in chequered esteem by society, which has attempted to repress, constrain and degrade its power. Daydreaming is considered unproductive, funding is funnelled away from the arts, and we've almost lost the concept of a visionary as anything other than a rich Technology CEO. One thing we can determine is that anything this maligned must be very powerful.

In fact, more and more academics are proposing that it is our capacity for imagination that specifically makes us human. Anthropologist Agustín Fuentes argues that the ability to imagine and to take that imagination and make it into reality is one of the things that is *really* distinctive about humans.[11] Clive Gamble, author of *Settling the Earth: The Archaeology of Deep Human History*,[12] argues that our ability to imagine other worlds was what led humans towards global expansion and exploration. 'Rather than being coldly rational, our pioneering ancestors were warmly relational – making connections between people, places and things. It was out of that imaginative mix that looking further than the horizon became attractive.'

Sir Ken Robinson goes even further, saying, 'Imagination, I believe, is what fundamentally sets us apart from the rest of life on earth – very little does, truthfully.'[13]

With that in mind, it's important that we respect and use this incredible capacity in a way that honours our humanity; that serves both us and the world.

That means calling time if the main use of your imagination is to indulge in endless worrying, conjuring your own personal disaster scenario at every junction of uncertainty in your life. Our bodies can't tell the difference between a genuine threat and a mental movie. Ever had that experience of dreaming that you fought with someone, only to wake up and still be mad at them over the breakfast table? Or does imagining some scenarios bring tears to your eyes, and leave your body feeling tight and your breath constricted, even though the reality is that right now, things are pretty damn good?

When I was a little girl, I discovered this peculiar way that your emotions and body can react to what you think about, not just what's actually going on. I was in a classroom and seeing me sobbing the teacher came over to ask if I was okay. I brightened up and said proudly, 'Yes, I just worked out I can make myself cry!' 'Oh,' she replied. 'How did you do that?' 'I imagined my whole family was murdered,' I told her. I think they spoke to my mum that day.

Toxic dreams and fighting ghosts

As someone who carried this vivid imagination into adulthood, I realize it's not as easy as just 'stopping worrying'. However, three realizations helped take the edge off this toxic habit.

The first was that far from preparing me for difficult situations in the future, it was actually lowering my self-esteem. I had come to believe that using my imagination to anticipate possible shortcomings or downfalls was helping me plan for the future and protect me from negative outcomes. There may have been times when it picked up a few possible threats. Most of the time, though, it just kept me locked in my own personal hellscape, and the damaging message that lay beneath these catastrophic imaginings was that I was not enough. Not strong enough, not powerful enough, not clever enough to respond to whatever came up in life in real time, without going through this imaginary over-preparation first. There came a point where my mental insurance was too expensive. Instead, I now use uncertainty as a chance to practise self-belief – to trust in myself that whatever happens I have enough, I know enough, I am enough, to take the right course of action in any given situation.

The second realization was that a not-so-useful arrogance was propelling this activity. I had inflated my power in worrying – playing a kind of impotent 'I told you so' game with myself, where I would select only the negative and then tell myself, 'Oh, look, bad things happened, therefore I was right to worry.' I would also tell myself, 'Oh, everything turned out great, therefore I was right to worry; it probably saved the situation.'

This rationale is illustrated wonderfully in a story involving a train, two men and toilet paper. A backpacker gets on a train in India, where he witnesses an old man, as soon as they leave the station, reach down into his shopping and take out a toilet roll. The old man then stands up, opens the window, and begins to tear off sheet after sheet, posting it through the window as the train flies through the countryside. The tourist watches him do this for fifteen minutes without interruption. But as he nears his stop, he summons up the courage to ask the man why he has been engaged in this bizarre activity. 'I'm stopping elephants from crossing the tracks,' says the old man. 'How can that stop the elephants?' the traveller replies. 'Well, have you seen an elephant yet?' is the response.

That's the thing about worry rituals – we think they help, but the reality is they're doing nothing but have us buy into an illusion of control. The price for that illusion is feeling tight and suspicious much of the time. Pretty rubbish deal, right?

Messy environments can produce more creative thought than neat and orderly ones. One experiment showed that people in disorderly environments tended to be more creative and think outside the box more. However, if you want to try *clean eating* or be more conscientious, the opposite is true – more orderly environments are beneficial.[14]

This worry ritual is observed especially when it comes to one particular preoccupation I call 'fighting ghosts'. These are imaginary arguments, a peculiar fusion of words, characters and pictures, that allow us to fight with our projections of people. I can't count the number of ghosts I've fought over the years – I regularly used to spend the bus ride to work having imaginary arguments with my boss, old boyfriends or colleagues, anticipating things they might say or do and my rejoinder to those things. It is, for the most part, not only a monumental waste of time and energy, but also brings out the worst in ourselves and others. When we expect others to attack us, it leaks into our attitude, behaviour and tone. We end up walking round covered in spikes, defensive and offensive, and resentful at things that haven't even happened yet. So if you spend any of your time fighting ghosts, stop it now. Stop cultivating a superpower that activates people's lowest common denominator. When it comes to relationships, very rarely can you solve a problem that hasn't happened yet.

The truth is, the majority of your worry is not only useless, but fosters a self-perception that is both simultaneously arrogant and insecure.

Working with your imagination

So, what to do instead? Well, the mind doesn't like emptiness, so it's very hard to rid it of an imagined grim scenario without replacing it with something else. So how about instead of imagining what you *don't want*, imagine what you *do want*?

This was my third realization: I could ask myself what would be the ideal scenario instead. I would begin just by posing the question: if I could make anything happen, what would it be? What do I really want? Once I had a starting point, I'd begin fleshing out the details – I use the word flesh on purpose – get visceral with it. Imagine what you would be seeing, hearing, feeling. See if you can get really specific. And then make it vivid, turning the colours up, the volume up. Make it as real as possible. Almost live it.

Sometimes it's hard to actually pinpoint what I want – and that's a humbling experience: to realize that I'm so focused on the scenario I *don't want* to play out that I forget to get in touch with what I hope will happen. It's like trying to use a map which only has where you *don't want to go* marked on it – it's impossible to navigate – and your focus is constantly pulled to the very thing you actually want to avoid.

Other times, I build these imaginary empires in my mind but it's hard for the feelings to come. I begin to think to myself: 'I wonder if I actually want this – I'm not actually feeling very excited.' Then I start to imagine something else and there's a lot of emotion that comes up. That's when I think, 'Wow, there's something for me here.' Even if the first is a five-star Caribbean holiday and the second is going home for a week to see the dogs.

Now, I'm not saying that you should never pay attention to these worst-case scenarios served up by your imagination, particularly if you're a firefighter, a doctor or a schoolteacher, or your job depends on risk assessment. What I am saying is that we use these imaginings either to create a safety net for ourselves or to turn that fear around to show us what we truly love and want to aim for. Try this: when you go to bed tonight, imagine all the things you want to happen in your life – the ideal scenarios. Paint them as vividly as possible, with lots of detail.

There's one last thing that's absolutely key when it comes to how we use our imagination, and that's the ability it gives us to put ourselves in a different position and see things from a different perspective. It allows us to empathize with others, to try and understand how other people might be feeling by imagining ourselves in that situation. This ability is vital for forming connections with other people – which is where caring about yourself becomes really challenging – in relationships.

Relationships

GIVE A F**K ABOUT RELATIONSHIPS

It's hard to give a f★★k about anything effectively if you don't also care about relating to people. There are seven billion people in the world. You are going to bump into them. Might as well learn how to bump into them so that everyone gets the most out of the experience.

'Bump' is a good word for it. Relationships are not always easy to navigate – we clash, fight and cry. That's why there's a lot in this section that deals with, shall we say, euphemistically, the 'tricky' parts of relating. (For 'tricky' read often screaming-into-the-sky-with-frustration.) To care about relationships in a way that helps us expand as people and get the loving connections we crave, we need to know first how to set boundaries, how to say no, how to avoid blame and how to be truthful with one another; caring about your connections in such a way that you don't abandon your own needs or demonize others' desires is a practice, and it's not about perfection. It's a bit like yoga – you do it, even though at first it might be uncomfortable and you feel like a fool and it sure as hell stretches you. The rewards are worth it, though.

We need people and we need relationships. Lord knows, I've tried to do life without intimacy, without close friends, without partnerships or passion. I've even tried to keep love at a distance, simply because I didn't know how to care without every quarrel, misunderstanding and separation overwhelming – and devastating – my whole life and my heart along with it.

But life without relationships is like profiteroles without delicious chocolate sauce: dry, bland and chewy. Humans are social creatures – we've evolved to connect and be with each other; it gives us something we yearn for as people, a special nutrient for survival that we can't access alone. Relationships are the lubricant that help make life more than a series of interesting events. They call us out to engage with the wider world, and make both our internal and external experiences brighter, more vivid, more alive – even if sometimes that intensity feels excruciating.

You can't do relationships without the risk of pain – all you can do is learn how to keep yourself safe and care about learning from those experiences. Not in a kind of 'never again with them' way (although that might be the case sometimes), but rather to teach you about yourself and how to connect with love.

Personal relationships are great for growth. They allow us to see our raw, sore spots, the places we still won't accept ourselves, where we project our judgements onto others and where we withdraw our love or friendship. If we can stay alert, we will also be shown situations that trigger us, where we still knee-jerk and lash out with fear, rather than being vulnerable, honest and sinking into love. It's only by seeing this that we can change things. Intimacy – being in close contact with people – can polish us, sloughing off our rough edges and transforming us from rough-hewn granite into shiny, smooth, beautiful pebbles.

For me, pride was one of the first things to be sanded off, along with a need to be always right. Relationships are ripe with opportunities for mistake-making, which is wonderful for taking the ego out of the driving seat, and useful because f★★king things up gives you an opportunity to get really good at making amends again. It also gives you a chance to practise forgiveness, and notice the places where your heart is still a bit hard, and closed off to love.

BOUNDARIES

Ever met one of those people who doesn't respect personal space? They always seem to corner you at parties. You strike up a conversation but they're leaning so far in that you edge away to feel comfortable, only to have them bend towards you again. Before you know it, you're doing this shuffling dance around the entire room, feeling vaguely invaded, until you mercifully bump into the drinks table and conjure a swift excuse to escape.

This is a small-scale example of what happens when

boundaries are not respected, or communicated; discomfort, collision and ultimately, disconnection.

Boundaries are fundamental to how we relate. They mark our limits: where we end and the other person begin and vice versa. They can be physical or spatial – like the earlier example. They can be emotional or mental – the appropriate separation of our feelings, thoughts and opinions. Boundaries are usually consciously set in romantic relationships. For example, in a monogamous pairing you might agree to be sexually intimate only with your current partner (the 'exclusive' chat) until you both decide otherwise. There are boundaries around property: this is my land; that is yours. We have boundaries around our bodies: people aren't allowed to touch us if we don't want them to. Importantly, the last two are examples of boundaries protected by law. In this section I'm talking about less clear-cut cases, but make no mistake, our boundaries are vital.

In relationships, clear boundaries help define what the other person can expect from you, and what you can expect from the other person. Your own boundaries form the bottom line of what you will and won't accept, based on what you need to feel free, safe and fulfilled.

Boundaries are something of a paradox. Far from separating us, the act of dividing what's yours and what's mine actually creates more intimacy, not less. Healthy boundaries strengthen the connection between people, allowing them to communicate more effectively and work together smoothly. Clear boundaries encourage people to take responsibility for themselves, to develop their own sense of self in security. Boundaries delineate the rules of engagement, providing a safe structure to allow people to move closer to each other. Without healthy boundaries, people feel invaded, resentful, they disengage and burn out.

This is a highly charged and delicate topic – failing to respect boundaries leaves us feeling violated, yet often we aren't taught about them and struggle to identify our own boundaries until they are crossed. We don't always know how to communicate boundaries effectively – and even when they are communicated, we fail to honour them with our actions. Plus, our boundaries are different with different people; there's no fixed set of rules that we can learn to avoid making mistakes. To top it all off, boundaries *shift* – both in individual relationships and within ourselves. It's not easy to keep up!

First, don't beat yourself up if you discover you've either disrespected your own boundaries or those of others. In the tectonic world of boundaries we are all violators and have been violated. Setting and respecting personal boundaries is my personal kryptonite – and here are some examples of where mine get fuzzy:

- *'Yes, it is totally fine to turn up late for our coffee date every time and no, I won't say anything.'*
- *'Sure, you can email me out of hours in a demanding tone and I will always respond.'*
- *'Yes, I'll come over and babysit for free even though I'm late on this work deadline and your child is a horror.'*

- 'Okay, Mum. You can turn up at my house without asking and then decide to clean it.' ('Oh, you didn't want me to tidy up all your personal papers without asking; I'm so sorry.')
- 'Oh, should I have asked before I brought my partner to dinner too?'
- 'I thought it was fine that I borrowed your top; it didn't seem like you really wore it that much.'

Maybe these scenarios feel familiar to you? If you want to build satisfying and nourishing relationships, you *need* to care about boundaries. Set your boundaries too loose and you'll end up doing way too much, worn out and tired with no energy for things you want to achieve. (People who can't say 'no', I'm looking at you.) If we don't know how to set boundaries, sometimes we end up building walls around us, which let no one in and, hello, isolation and loneliness (people who struggle to say yes).

How to spot if you struggle with boundaries:
- *Are you often late?*
- *Do you often find yourself overly irritated by others' lateness?*
- *Do you often feel tired and like you have no time for yourself?*
- *Do you flake on people at the last minute?*
- *Do you ever 'ghost' dates?*
- *Do you frequently shut people out or ignore them?*
- *Do you ever feel responsible for someone else's happiness?*

- *Do you think if someone else is unhappy it is 'your job' to make them feel better?*
- *Do you ever attribute your unhappiness to someone else?*
- *Have you ever been accused of oversharing or interfering?*
- *Do you find it impossible to maintain or share your good mood if someone around you is in a bad mood?*
- *Do you feel other people's feelings are more important than your own?*
- *Do you rarely lose your temper but when you do, you explode?*
- *Do you feel constantly wracked by feelings of guilt?*
- *Do you feel like the only safe place for you to relax is when you are on your own?*

If you said yes to two or more of these, it might be that you have some confusions around boundaries. What should help your relationships be less climactic and more connected is establishing what is your responsibility, what is not, and learning how to say 'no'. I'll cover all this in the following sections.

Knowing what's yours

For a long time, I had zero emotional boundaries. I might have been walking around masquerading as a separate human being – with my own feelings, dreams, problems and needs – but actually I was just a super-sensitive radio tower, humming with everyone else's music. If they were happy, I was happy. If they were sad, I was disturbed. I only conceptually understood the phrase 'not my problem' – if it was within my radius, it would nag for my attention until I became involved. I internalized the needs of others – it felt like my job to make everyone get along. Only then did I feel settled.

When you struggle with boundaries it becomes difficult to work out what's yours and what belongs to other people.

Though the concept of personal boundaries is nothing new (think of the Bible on personal responsibility – 'you reap what you sow'), it's only really been popular as part of counselling or self-help work since the 1980s.

Do you have some days where you wake up and it's as if you've forgotten to put your skin on? When every single emotion you come into contact with – from reading an angry post on Facebook to an upset friend on the phone – jangles your entire system, until by the end of the day, you feel overwhelmed, heavy and you're not really sure why? It's like you're a tuning fork for dozens of dissonant emotional vibrations that you can't seem to shut out, and so you just reverberate into the ground and then shut down, exhausted.

Your feelings are your feelings – their feelings are their feelings

Each of us is ultimately responsible for how we feel. What we tell ourselves, how we interpret situations and how we respond to whatever is going on is what causes us to feel the way we do.

If we're stressed by a deadline – that's our stress. No one planted the feelings in our body. If we're happy – that's ours, too; we showed up and allowed ourselves to feel free. If we're upset, that's our emotional processes at work – it's not someone else's job to reverse the event to make our feelings change. If we feel guilty about the way someone else feels – that's our guilt. No one 'made' you feel anything and neither are you solely responsible for anyone else's emotional turbulence.

Our feelings are directed by our own deeply personal inner processes. People can feel differently about the same events, depending on their past history, their beliefs, their mood that day.

But what about upsetting people? Well, it happens. You can't control that, but you can adjust what you make it mean about you as a person, or how you respond to having accidentally hurt someone's feelings. Just say what's true for you at any given moment and let people react how they wish. They are allowed to feel how they want to, too. It's their life and their experience. Respect that.

Getting in touch with yourself

It's human to sympathize but it isn't healthy to take on everybody else's feelings as your own. For a start, it's exhausting: we have enough trouble processing our own emotions without having to work through a ghostly imprint of everyone else's, too. Even if you're not conscious of doing it, you may begin to feel crazy because you feel awful but can't identify why – plus there's not very much you can do about adjusting those negative emotions, because they weren't even yours to begin with.

Extreme emotional contagion is actually the death of compassion. It may lead to resentment, as you forget that someone in pain isn't demanding you to experience their pain, too. You might isolate yourself, because being around groups of people is too much with all their different feelings, problems and needs. Or maybe you develop a need to control people and situations excessively to maintain a sense of your own equilibrium.

This is the dark side to not having appropriate emotional boundaries. If you need other people to feel okay in order to feel okay yourself, then you are going to end up having to manipulate and suppress other people's feelings. It's not about sorting out the world so that you can feel good. It's about developing your own internal processes for feeling good and then bringing that joy to those bits of the world that want it.

It's easy to say, but if you've spent a large portion of your life being very good at watching and gauging other people's emotional states, you may have no idea how to feel your own emotions. You might be great at pleasing people or knowing their anger triggers, but there's a gaping void in the place of your personal feelings about an issue. You can change this; it just takes practice.

Start slow

Set an alarm on your phone three times a day, so that you can check in and ask yourself, 'How do I feel right now?' See if you can come up with two emotions and where you feel them in your body. If you can't name the feeling, just see if you can describe physical sensations. This process is important, even though it is hard at first, because if you are in touch with how your own feelings *feel* inside your body, it's easier to recognize when you're starting to take on an emotion that's not yours.

Your problems are your problems – their problems are their problems

This might sound harsh, but no one is obliged to solve your problems. No one has to listen to you and no one *has* to give you sympathy.

'Ah,' you might think, 'but what about my partner – surely I should expect them to cheer me up?'

Nope. It is not their duty to make you happy. It is no one's job to rescue you from your own life. You can tell them how you would like to be listened to and you can ask for advice or support, but it is their choice whether they decide to offer any. They might have had a bad day, too. They might need to attend to their own problems. You are both adults, even if that makes two grumpy adults sitting in silence, taking ten minutes to thaw out before they can be available for each other.

This might seem all very clinical, and it's important to note that there's nothing wrong with giving. You may enjoy giving. But look at your intention – why you're doing it. Giving out of guilt or obligation, because of a need for validation or with expectation of 'payback', are all manipulative recipes for resentment and low self-worth. Similarly, asking from a place of entitlement doesn't allow someone to freely give to you, or honour their ability to say no. Which leads on to the next point.

Your needs are your needs – their needs are their needs.

Taking responsibility for your needs means investigating what they are in good time, so that you can get them met from an appropriate source – the one most able to meet them – and before the requirement becomes pressing. It can be hard to ask for help, but it is the kindest thing you can do for yourself and others. Waiting until you are desperate to ask for help sets you up for rejection or suffering if someone exercises their right to say no. It is not a kind way to treat yourself or others. It's wise to attend to your needs as they arise – a little and often approach – rather than depriving yourself until your emotional world is exploding around you.

If someone says 'no' move on and keep asking. Remember, it's not about you personally. See your ability to receive a 'no' as empowering – it gives you permission to say 'no' when you are not able to say 'yes', and it's good practice: you were able to receive a 'no' and you didn't self-destruct. It doesn't change how valuable you are.

> The reason they tell you to fit your own oxygen mask first on a plane is because the drop in pressure means that in just a few minutes – perhaps before you have even helped someone else – your brain starts to stop functioning and cannot even identify basic shapes. You will then need someone else to help you or you will die.

Ask for help from the place or person that is most able to give you what you want. Stop asking your mum to help you with the thing she has proven herself historically to be bad at, then getting cross when she lets you down. Don't make demands on your partner for something when you know a friend is better at the listening and empathy you need. If one person can't help in the way that you need them to, you can ask someone else for the appropriate help. Your friend, mum, or partner might not be the right choice, but your doctor, solicitor or accountant might be.

You don't need to mould and shape yourself to every person that comes into your life in order to be liked. You have a right to be yourself, and to have that self feel safe and expressed, and have its needs met. You might not have been able to do that for yourself as a child, but you're an adult now. Reclaim what's yours, let go of what's not and leave others to do the same.

Boundary maintenance

Next time you are confronted with a situation where someone is feeling a very strong emotion and you are tempted to take it on yourself, take a deep breath and try this practice:

- *Stabilize yourself – feel your feet heavy on the floor; you can even imagine that roots come out of the soles of your feet down into the earth.*
- *Notice the other person's emotion – say to yourself 'he/she is feeling anxious today'. Remind yourself. 'That's theirs, they are feeling that. I am calm. I do not feel that.'*
- *Breathe. Notice your own emotional status, rather than getting on their rollercoaster.*
- *Remind yourself that the other person is allowed to ask for what they want if they need.*
- *Imagine covering yourself in clear, bright, gold light from your head to your feet: a force field of protection around you. Remain calm and do not mirror their emotion.*
- *After leaving their company check in with yourself and see how you feel. How much have you taken on? This takes practice to become automatic, so don't be discouraged if you find it hard.*

Saying 'no'

Fundamental to being human in relationship with other humans is acknowledging our limits: physical, emotional and mental. We have our own inner-boundary barometer, which lets us know what is acceptable to us or not. Sometimes our mental chatter interferes, telling us we should agree to something – it's polite, our egos think we can handle it, or we think it will be less hassle to just go along with it. However, our bodies always let us know the true answer. Whether we feel able, right or safe doing something is a far more primal question than is often acknowledged. Ignoring our limits is arrogant and abusive – both to oneself and to others.

If you can listen hard enough, and practise interpreting the signals given by your body, you'll learn to detect whether doing something is right for you or whether it is breaking a boundary. It happens almost on an energetic level. Over time I am learning to note what happens in my body when I am out of my depth and have gone too far, too fast. I get this shrinking, tight feeling in my upper body and a kind of numbness in my face, cold tingles in my belly. Occasionally, the sensation is very intense and I'll feel a jet stream of heat shoot up the front of my body.

This isn't hocus pocus – you can sense these boundaries in other people, too. It's the felt awareness of separation that can make it obvious someone isn't single or available for romance. It's why there are some friends you just don't get physically close to, or you might not naturally hug. We don't consciously choose not to touch or ask them out, it's just we can sense it wouldn't be appropriate, or there's some resistance from them to – like an invisible dividing line.

When we misinterpret or fail to listen to these signals, we only notice the existence of a boundary once it's been breached. If we are the violators, we may notice a reaction in the other person, and then we can apologize or take other necessary action to amend the wrong. If one of our boundaries is crossed, a feeling of resentment or abuse usually appears. With the exception of certain serious violations (rape, sexual assault, deliberate physical or emotional threat or abuse) that are prohibited by law, when this happens it's best to take what is happening seriously but avoid assigning blame. It is almost always as much your responsibility to protect, communicate and assert your boundary – and set consequences if that boundary is broken – as it is the other person's to respect it.

'No big deal'

Asserting little boundaries is as vital as putting in place those more definitive borders. We tend to forget these less obvious ones, persuading ourselves that we can or should put up with certain minor infractions, gritting our teeth and getting on with it when the person we sit next to at work leaves a mess all over our desk during the night shift. Or when our flatmate doesn't clean the bath. When our friend turns up half an hour late for coffee, then fails to apologize. If we can't tap all the emotion down, we might glare or act a little frosty, then moan to someone else later, but we still fail to address and provide an opportunity for resolving the misdemeanour.

These examples are all small things in the grand scheme. However, I find that every time I ignore the quiet voice inside me that says 'This is not acceptable to me', some tightness appears in my body. I swallow this little brick of resistance down, but it doesn't go away; it just sinks down and slides in neatly, Tetris-style, slotting in beside the last choked down 'no'. And so, bit by bit, unvoiced breach by unvoiced breach, a wall of anger builds inside me. Then I might go out for lunch and the kitchen gets my order wrong. I could assert myself calmly, but at this point I'm up to my throat in backed-up 'no's', at the absolute limit of what I can handle. So the poor waitress gets the full force of anger meant for other people as I spray a week's worth of resentment all over the restaurant.

Telling people, step by step, what is acceptable to you and what is not is a much kinder, more honest way to live, for everyone. Otherwise our lives fill up with things and we don't actually like or want a single one of them. It saps us of energy – living lives full of other people's junk simply because we didn't say 'no'.

It can be very tempting to drop everything to help someone every time a request is made – especially if you think that person is in a difficult place or needs you in some way. But you are not the only person in the world able to help and you are not a 'bad' person if you don't want to – especially if helping would have a direct negative impact on yourself. Obligation and good deeds don't combine well. One pollutes the other. It's the karmic equivalent of squirting ketchup into a nice hot bubble bath.

Linguists argue about whether in the English language yes or no should have a grammatical category all of their own. They are considered 'sentence words' – where a single word forms a sentence. However, some languages don't have yes or no – Irish Gaelic and Finnish, for example. In Finnish, if someone asked you 'Have you read the book?' you would simply reply 'I have read the book' or 'I have not read the book' – the positive or negative form of the verb is used. This is called an 'echo' response.

It's difficult to assert yourself – we fear falling short of someone's expectations. That's okay. Sometimes loving ourselves looks like disappointing other people. Saying no to what we don't want means we have the space to say yes to the things we do want. It creates the space for us to do those things with our whole heart. It requires using our voice and making sure our actions reflect our words.

Communicating a boundary

People are not mind readers. Just because something is okay with you, doesn't mean it is acceptable to someone else. It is down to us to communicate our boundaries, so that the other person is made aware, and we can avoid clogging up our consciousness with blame or shame.

Prior to the conversation, consider these things:

1. **Know what you want**

   These can be difficult interactions, so go into the conversation with a clear idea of what is needed and hold on to that anchor if emotions become heated.

   Example: I want my co-worker to stop leaving cups, papers and old tissues on my desk so that I don't have to clear them up in the morning.

2. **Know why you are having the conversation**

   Take a note of both the positive and negative reasons for setting the boundary. Sure, you don't want dirty mugs on your desk because it's irritating, but why else is it beneficial? To have a more respectful relationship with your colleague? To concentrate more on your work? Know the reasons it is important to you to have a clean desk. Turn any negatives into positives: it will put you into a more approachable mind-set and avoid unnecessary attacks.

   Example: 'I want there to be no mugs on my desk because I feel it's disrespectful if I have to clean it up' becomes 'I feel respected when my space is left clean.' 'I shouldn't have to start my day cleaning up rubbish' becomes 'I am able to

*get on with my work immediately.' 'I don't hate everyone'
becomes 'I feel more generous towards my colleagues.'*

3. **Find a neutral, private space to have the conversation**
   *Have the conversation in a place where both of you aren't
   going to feel under excess pressure — for example, less than
   ideal settings are in front of co-workers, in a very small room,
   or in a place where either of you feels defensive.*

4. **Starting the conversation**
   *State a value-neutral, fact-based description of the
   situation calmly. However riled up we may feel, it is
   crucial in these delicate moments to remove any overtly
   accusatory language.*

   *Example: 'When I come in every morning, there are a lot
   of coffee mugs and papers on my desk that are not mine.' Do
   not say: 'You leave all the mugs on my desk in the morning; it
   looks revolting and I should not have to deal with this sh★t.'*

5. **Say how it makes you feel**
   *Express your feelings. Do not qualify or apologize. Keep
   it simple. Inhale compassion and exhale anger. You dislike
   the activity of this person, not necessarily this person. It is
   unlikely the person is deliberately irritating (if they are; take
   comfort in the fact that they may have their own boundary
   issues and haven't yet found the courage to voice their
   issue with you). Sometimes we feel so defensive, we jump
   straight to attack mode. Sharing the truth underneath that
   layer of armament — that it is really difficult for you to
   say this, or that you feel hurt or disrespected, humanizes
   the conversation. Remember, however, to maintain your*

agency (your power). It's not about how they 'made' you feel. This is your boundary, your emotions and your responsibility.

   Example: 'This is difficult for me to say, but I feel annoyed and disrespected when I see mugs left on my desk. For me, someone respecting my space means they respect me, and so I get angry when I see them there.'

6. **State what you need in a clear and direct way**
   Example: 'I want to come in to a clean desk every morning and I would like it if you cleaned up anything you put there on the night shift before you go home.'

7. **State what this would give you**
   Example: 'This would let me get straight to work in the morning without delay. I value our relationship and this would help me work alongside you better, too.'

8. **State the consequences of breaking this boundary**
   Example: 'I want to give you fair warning that this is important to me and if it happens again I will ask to be moved.'

You want to give the other person a chance to honour your feelings, but you also want to show you are serious. Once a boundary is set, it is important to enforce the consequences of a boundary being broken – follow words with actions. It may feel extreme, but it shows self-respect.

Dealing with difficult reactions

Remember to set boundaries with love – limits are there to allow relationships to flourish, after all. A lot of the time, people don't realize the impact of their actions. If the boundary infraction has been going on for some time and you have not spoken up, then this may be a shock for the person listening.

Sometimes setting up a boundary may see the other person get defensive, angry or questioning. Though they are entitled to their anger, you are entitled to your boundary. Do not mirror their response or be intimidated by it; instead simply restate your boundary calmly, without capitulating or attending to their arguments. Signal that this is not a negotiation but rather the limit of what you find acceptable. Holding your ground calmly demonstrates that anger will not scare you into changing your mind.

Generally, boundary-setting conversations tend to happen on an ad-hoc basis, i.e. when they are crossed. Expressly communicating them can be anxiety-inducing, but setting and maintaining boundaries and learning how to handle people who fail to respect them gets easier and helps you protect your self-esteem.

OWNING YOUR PART

Everyone's keen to brag about their relationships when things are going smoothly. Instagram is full of kissing couples, cosy beach snaps and #besties. Less popular is taking a share of responsibility when things get messy. Then, in the privacy of WhatsApp or behind closed doors, tempers flare, events are dissected, and accountability is tossed like a hot potato. You'll usually hear blame 'You're wrong', victimhood 'Why do you always do this to me?' or shame (nothing at all – shame gets off on silence, disconnection and withdrawal). It's natural to find yourself in one of these emotional pedal bins when events go pear-shaped. Upon noticing, though, it's wise to get yourself the hell out of there. Blame, shame and victimhood are all enemies of intimacy. They are blinding and suffocating forces, robbing us of insight, personal power and connection.

That doesn't mean disagreements won't happen. Relationships that exist without any conflict are not relationships, merely two people who occasionally exist side by side. Close contact between two things generates friction. That's okay. This friction, or conflict, by which I mean anything from disagreement to a full-on verbal fight, is a natural and necessary part of intimacy and personal growth, yet we run from it as if it's a threat to ourselves and our connections. It doesn't have to be that way. The way we approach conflicts can make our relationships stronger. It's like *Super Mario Land* on Gameboy: we're navigating through a series of fights and challenges that allow the relationship to move up a level.

Conflicts within relationships mainly result in disconnection for one reason: people refuse, either consciously or unconsciously, to take responsibility for how they contributed to the situation in question. As relationships are co-created between two or more people, so too is the conflict that's sometimes generated within them. The root of the word conflict comes from Latin, '*con*' (with) and '*fligere*' (to strike) – or to strike together. My point is that there is always a part that you will have played to contribute to the current situation – even unintentionally, or by omission. Perhaps it was by not saying something or not doing something, making an assumption, breaking an unstated boundary, or being unclear, but if it happened in a relationship, there is a place you can take responsibility, too. Owning your part is not about right or wrong or about fault; it's about accountability. It's saying, 'Yes, I did that and I can see now how *that* may have led to *that*.'

This is important because unless both people can own their part in the discord, it's hard for either side to offer or receive a true apology; to cultivate forgiveness and move the relationship forward. Without this willingness to examine what went wrong, how all parties co-conspired to create it, and a clear commitment to handling circumstances differently, it's hard for trust to be rebuilt.

This, like most things, is easier said than done. Sometimes, a sense of stubbornness and misplaced pride means we refuse to take responsibility for our part in the drama unless the person we're in conflict with takes responsibility for theirs. This is not only childish, but denies us the benefits of taking responsibility, which are available whether or not the other person decides to join in the fun.

By owning your part, the first advantage you get to pile

on your personal-development plate is power. Admitting you either chose or caused a situation, at least in part, means you're back in the driving seat of your own life. You're recognizing that you have power and that chaos is not just randomly happening all around you without you (subconsciously) sanctioning it! Being able to meet someone as an accountable adult is an incredibly important part of having a relationship – the counter position meaning that any interactions are simply coming *at* you and happening *to* you, rather than *with* you. It leaves you left to navigate a power dynamic rather than a relationship.

Second, investigating how you could have contributed to a set of circumstances and seeing how something you did created a result you didn't like will provide you with helpful self-knowledge. Conflict is wonderful for providing insight into our own blind spots – things that other people know about us but that we don't know about ourselves. This can be uncomfortable – discovering that we display arrogance or that we frequently mislead people is not an easy process. We've hidden these traits from ourselves for a reason after all – we don't want to see what's there! Claiming these 'secret', abandoned bits of ourselves is actually the loving thing to do, however. It allows us to develop self-respect and gives us a better chance of maintaining deeper connections because we can now truly bring all parts of ourselves into a relationship. Plus, more generally, we're less likely to go around unintentionally flinging unclaimed parts of our personality everywhere, which, I promise, as someone who's discovered pockets of arrogance, disdain, superiority and collusion in her own abandoned soul suitcase, benefits no one.

We are far more likely to hold people responsible for negative actions than positive ones, assigning them credit or praise. Essentially, the worse the action, the more likely we are to think that the person intended for it to happen, rather than it being unfortunate, or mere bad luck. We think of blame and praise as being two sides of the same coin, but they really aren't. They are actually completely different processes in the brain; blame sees activity in the amygdala – the emotional part of the brain – whereas praise or credit is assigned in a more logical part of the brain. Just something to watch out for – especially if you're on a jury.[15]

These (free!) personal-development delights are available to you whether the other person wants to own their part or not. Something funny happens when you go and make yourself vulnerable in this way, though. Suddenly, as you admit what you did, everything softens, and they can see their part, too. Even more magically, they are also willing to own up to it.

Swallowing your ego is a bit like when you drink a cup of baking soda and warm water for a stomach ache: it's initially deeply unpleasant and makes you feel a bit sick, but you feel so much better afterwards. Promise. As Raylan Givens says in the TV series *Justified*: 'If you run into an asshole in the morning, you ran into an asshole. If you run into assholes all day, you're the asshole.' If there's one thing owning your part helps with, it's being less of an asshole. And when you've indulged in some asshole behaviour, admit it, learn from it, and love yourself anyway.

How to give a good apology

The most healing kind of apology to both give and receive are ones where someone doesn't just say they are sorry, but explains *why* they are sorry. The more specific someone can be, the better. It allows the person receiving it to feel heard and felt and both parties to move on from the event with some resolution from the situation. For example:

> '*I'm sorry for raising my voice the way I did. I can see how that wasn't easy for you, that it didn't help me get my point across and why your feelings are now hurt.*'

It can be humbling to do this, but it's also incredibly freeing.

GETTING OFF YOUR HIGH HORSE

Being on my high horse has been my favourite way to absolve myself of accountability. The ease of putting all the responsibility on someone else, before riding off, morally righteous, in a sunset of blissful impotence, is wonderfully satisfying to my ego.

Though being astride your high horse might give you a feeling of immense power and righteousness, paradoxically, due to the very nature of the beast, it means you are simultaneously declaring yourself a helpless victim.

My high horse is called Veronica. She is particularly vocal when it comes to men, and is rather dominant when first dates go poorly. When it comes to disagreements with co-workers, family or partners, she casts herself in a saintly hue, all the while heaping blame onto others. She loves contradictions, too. I think the most absurd story I've heard her tell is that all my dates were going badly because I was too strong and powerful. 'Isn't it awful that all men are so intimidated by beauty and talent? Poor me, there's nothing I can do . . .' was her favourite story for a while. You can always tell when someone is on their high horse – they speak of being wronged, but they make very strange-looking victims.

My wonderful friends call me out when Veronica's around because, although they love my headstrong side, they also know it doesn't serve me or the situation well. There are two reasons I am able to get off my high horse when my friends call me out. The first is that I gave my horse a name so I don't identify it with my true self any more – it's a pattern; it's not me – and therefore letting go of 'having to be right' is that bit easier if they talk about Veronica, rather than Felicity. The second is that I can feel how much they love me, and they will give me attention and hear me out whether I'm distressed because I'm morally right or because I made a mistake. One of the payoffs for sharing a story where you are dramatically wronged is receiving sympathy and attention. If I know I am going to receive that anyway, then the motivation for me to continue with my victim story is less compelling. They have been there through enough f★★k-ups of my own contriving – I know now that they will love me whatever.

I'm glad I have friends that can help me down from my high horse with love, excruciating though it is sometimes. Being right is very comforting, but in the long term it's likely to be the only sop you're left with. Being on your high horse is a swift canter to loneliness and misery. It has a short shelf-life with most people and it can make you behave like a demanding toddler.

Someone refusing to come off their high horse is so afraid of failure, rejection and being wrong that they can only tolerate acquiescence to their point of view. Even if the person who challenges their version of events isn't the same individual who is initially believed to have wronged them, they often will not allow their powerfully stated victimhood to be disputed. In fact, daring to dispute their version of events can sometimes have them ride higher, as you, too become part of their proof that they are indeed wronged as you refused to take them seriously!

When someone regularly engages in this kind of victimhood, they tend to try and find someone else who is astride a victimhood high horse about the same thing, whom they can prance about in ever decreasing circles. This is called collusion. I'm somewhat embarrassed to say I used to do this. A lot. In fact, I set up my social circle in such a way that I knew particular friends would collude with me on certain things and I could tap up people accordingly, depending on whatever it was I wanted sympathy for.

If I was having a problem with my boss, I'd ring the friend who I knew would let me play moral superior there, because she had similar issues with her manager. If I wanted to rant about dating, I'd message a friend who I knew would back up my story that my lack of success was nothing to do with me but about everyone else.

If you recognize yourself here – if you've colluded or sought collusion – stop it, it's not kind and it's not helpful. Being on a high horse keeps the rider a prisoner of a place they don't like. It enables someone to keep doing the same thing over and over even though it's giving them undesirable results. It keeps them stuck in a mind-set where they tell themselves they have no power over their own life or relationships. You're confirming a story that hurts – either them or you. If you're on your high horse, it's time to dismount, meet someone face to face, one human being to another, and reconnect on a more equal footing.

VICTIMHOOD

When we adopt a victim 'mentality', we *perceive* whatever is happening in our life as occurring through forces beyond our control. Despite us being at the centre of the drama, we absolve ourselves of all responsibility and insist we have no power to change anything. In victimhood, all focus is on the powerlessness of the wounded self, a kind of 'life is pain' attitude. *Victimhood* may display itself as resignation, a kind of sad stoicism or woeful helplessness.

I'm using the word victimhood instead of victim, because a victim is someone who is genuinely harmed and adversely affected by forces *outside their control*. For them the term 'victim' is not a mind-set, it's a statement of reality. Victimhood, meanwhile, is when someone has adopted a perception of the world where they are *always* a victim: it's their general outlook rather than confined to a temporary event. You can certainly be a victim of something; you cannot be, unconditionally, a victim. We are human beings: we are not prey and we are not enduringly powerless, even though sometimes it may feel that way.

Someone who is trapped in victimhood is likely to experience a lot of drama in their lives, which they believe is nothing to do with them. Rather, the turmoil is coming 'at' them for no reason other than their own bad luck, a series of unfortunate things happening 'to' them. The world can be unfair – and it is, frequently – but the important thing is what we do next. Someone in victimhood is stuck feeling disempowered; rather than able to captain their own existence, they are beset with problems. They cannot see that these problems could be in part a consequence of their own thoughts, actions or feelings. They may seem dedicated to a pessimistic view of the world – at times it might even feel that they are getting off on being miserable.

If dealing with someone like this sounds draining, that's because it is. Regular conversations with someone in a victim mind-set feels like being assaulted with relentless negativity. On top of that, people who feel they have been wronged aren't always the most compassionate souls when it comes to letting a bit of attention and love flow the other way. A Stanford University study connected the feeling of being wronged with behaving less generously towards others.[16] When participants were asked to recall a time when they were treated unfairly, right before being asked to help others complete a simple task, they were more likely to refuse than another group of participants, who were asked to recall a time they were bored. The unlikeable side effects of dealing with someone in victimhood aside, it's important not to slip into judgement yourself.

For a start, we all do this from time to time. When it comes to personal responsibility, or hauling ourselves out of a hole, sometimes we choose to dodge the uncomfortable bullet of doing the difficult, proactive thing and instead claim to be powerless or that matters are simply hopeless. More than once have I swooned on the sofa in victim mode, and a small degree of wallowing (I time myself now – I'm allowed to hide under the duvet for a half an hour pretending that me putting on weight, or someone postponing a meeting or criticizing me, is the worst thing ever) never injured anyone. We're allowed to have hurt feelings and attend to those. It might not be a big deal, you might know you'll get another job interview or date or that it's simply your ego that's sore, but it still feels rotten, and that's okay.

If you're a friend witnessing this, be careful and pay close attention. What might *look* like victimhood could be someone sinking into depression and needing proper mental-health treatment. If someone is so high up in anxiety that they can't see the wood for the trees, and their body has gone into fight or flight response, that needs to be soothed with slow breathing, gentle attention and calming words before any kind of conversation can take place.

Even if that's not the case, blame someone for 'being a victim' and you are simply boxing them back into that mentality. (You're also getting a little on your high horse yourself.) People do not adopt this mind-set consciously, and often it is learnt from childhood. Perhaps this was how they saw their mother and father talk about the world. Perhaps in their family they had to be sick, upset or unfortunate before they were able to get genuine attention from their parents, be listened to and have their needs met.

Victimhood may also be driven by anxiety – fear of failure, abandonment or wrongdoing. Sometimes people feel that if they admit to a mistake, they risk losing the love and respect of their peers. They might believe people will leave them unless they make themselves so pitiful that others feel they have to stay. There are benefits to this 'poor me' mind-set: it often means others actively avoid criticizing or upsetting you as you are already sad.

Some people feel that if they are the victim of misfortune, they can demand certain treatment or claim they have a 'right' to certain things. People may struggle to assert themselves, cope with criticism, or ask for what they want based purely on their own intrinsic value as humans. This sounds like a damning diagnosis, but the reality is, we all find ourselves here from time to time – I've definitely pulled a few puppy-dog eyes in my life, or overdramatized a mildly uncomfortable situation to get the sympathy I want from friends – then convincing myself that is the reality. It reminds me of 'the last brownie' game in the film *Notting Hill* – where each character has to paint their life's woes in such a pitiful hue that the diners feel sorry for them and give them the last piece of cake at supper. We all naturally step into victimhood at times, it just becomes damaging when we stay there – or we are less conscious of doing it and think we genuinely have no power.

For someone in whom victimhood is deeply entrenched, therapy will be the only long-term solution. However, if there is a specific situation with a friend, partner or family member, these five steps have served to help me.

1. ***Can you approach this with empathy?***
    If you don't feel like you have the patience, energy or neutrality to communicate clearly and compassionately

with the individual when they speak like this, it is better to realize this, withdraw and set up boundaries. Otherwise you risk fuelling the fire and causing upset for both of you.

2. **Set up boundaries**

You are not obliged to help the person, solve their problems or give them attention. Remember, your first responsibility is to yourself. Decide what you are willing or able to give and set up a boundary. For example, you might say: 'Just to let you know, I can only listen for five minutes.' Or perhaps: 'I can hear you are hurt and upset and I'm sorry about that. I actually have some things going on right now and I'm not able to listen, but come back to me later when you are ready to talk solutions.'

3. **Listen and repeat it back**

This is an active listening technique which helps reflect back to the person in victimhood how dramatic they might be being as well as helping them feel heard, which is helpful if what they need is attention. For example, if they say, 'I am fighting with my partner and it's just unbearable and the end of the world right now', you might respond: 'Okay, so I understand: your partner is angry at you and it feels unbearable and like the world is ending – is that right?' Don't react, just stay very calm and repeat back what they are saying. Don't get drawn into offering solutions.

4. **Accept their version of events**

Don't challenge, but gently ask questions. Accept what is going on for them, that things are bad. Then ask, 'So what do you want to do about that?' If they say, 'I can't do *anything' just accept that and say, 'Okay, then. Guess there's nothing anyone can do.' Take their version of events as it is; don't engage or try to get them to see it another way yet. You want them to focus on how they would like to respond to it. Other questions like 'What would the most powerful version of yourself do in this situation?' can also help them think in ways that remove them from that mind-set. Or you might try, 'In an ideal world, what would you do next?' You can even ask: 'What's one thing you could do for yourself right now to feel better?' Then follow up with: 'And how can you make that happen?'*

5. ***Invite them to make a change***

   After they have identified one thing they might want to do to alleviate their negative feelings or move towards a solution, say you have an invitation for them, and ask if they would like to hear it. You can say something like, 'My invitation to you would be for you to take this step forward right now – would you be willing to do that?' Whatever their answer is, accept it, and draw the conversation to a close. If their answer is no, you can say, 'Okay, great, well thanks for brainstorming all the same', or something that doesn't attempt to take responsibility for their change.

Remember to set your own boundaries. If someone is in victimhood and you want to help them out, empathy and listening go a long way. It doesn't mean you have to confirm their point of view is correct, but you can allow them to feel heard and don't try to 'fix' them; that's not your responsibility and just removes more agency from them. Be careful, too, that you don't leap into judgement or tell them to snap out of it. It's possible to be so fixated on not indulging victimhood that you ignore genuine issues that need resolution and attention from external sources. People can have legitimate complaints and need genuine support. It might be an employee raising a concern about a certain process in the company. Even if it isn't, remember that the person's pain is real for them, and perspective is hard to come by when you're upset. Frankly, when we're down an emotional hole, we often need a hand up to see that there is a way out – even (and perhaps especially) if it's a hole of our own making. Being an adult – rather than a wounded child – is not an easy switch to make. We all find ourselves regressing and it's wise to remember that. Talking to someone in victimhood requires a great deal of patience and sensitivity as well as an acute alertness to whether there is a legitimate issue that needs listening and attending to, victim mentality or not.

BLAME

Blame is an ugly little bridge troll that feeds our lack: lack of self-esteem, lack of trust and lack of power. It wills on our worst feelings and grows fat on our scarcity. Blame is cheap these days. They say sex sells, but it is fear and judgement that *really* make people spend money. Trust me, I've worked in newspapers. Blame-generated anger and petitions for punishment is the media's bread and butter. Politics really gets off on blame, too.

Doesn't it make you mad? No wonder we're all so quick to do it. It's almost definitely all their fault the country is in the state it's in. They should be made to pay for their actions, shouldn't they?

And that's the thing about blame … it's so easy to fall into. Blame generates more blame, ping-ponging anger and hurt back and forth, making the emotional divide between us greater and greater, and moving further and further from the original issue.

It puts blinkers on us and makes a person the problem, rather than a situation. It is narrow-minded and seeks retribution rather than resolution. And so we get stuck in a blame cycle.

There are a few assumptions that drive blame. The first is this notion we are always consciously able to choose our actions based on the outcome we want.

When we blame, we assume people could have anticipated the negative consequences of their actions and despite being able to choose a different option, for some mysterious reason (we usually fill in the blanks here and say it's because they are a bad person) they did not do the 'correct' thing.

The truth is, most of the time, people are doing the best they can with the hand of cards they are playing. It's just we all start with a slightly different hand. Assume the person you're tempted to blame had a good reason for saying what they said or doing what they did. Their choices were either logical or hard to avoid, given their mind, their unique set of beliefs and history.

If you could slide perfectly into their shoes, their behaviour wouldn't seem unreasonable. It's just a matter of vantage point and knowing what's occupying their vision, activating those thoughts and feelings, and directing their decisions at that time. Blame is really just a perspective problem.

This doesn't stop people from taking responsibility for their actions, but should remove the layer of judgement that often comes with it. The castigation, accusation and hectoring that comes with blame is usually unhelpful. Instead of passive-aggressive punishment, it's far easier to analyse the situation together, with an open attitude of acceptance. Posing questions that widen someone's perspective and empowering them, providing them with tools and knowledge so that they can choose more positively next time, is a more effective route – both in work and home relationships.

Simple causes for complex events

When we blame, we assume that every event has a sole cause and that we must know what or who that is – and right away. Sometimes, there does seem to be an obvious trigger, but life is rarely that elementary. This desire to find a singular simple cause for complex occurrences is an attempt to stem the fear of losing control when faced with life's unknowable forces. However, blame is an ineffective tool for dealing with the uncertainty of existence. It's like trying to cookie-cutter a blossom tree.

Instead of trying to force things to be more mechanistic, pretending life can be predicted, we would be better off spending our time learning how to embrace uncertainty. So some things happened that we didn't expect or necessarily want – how can we see that as an opportunity? Could it be that these situations are a perfect place to test our self-belief and assurance in ourselves, and reaffirm that we are okay not always knowing? Perhaps we can use these moments to learn more – to go to the heart of things and really pick apart what made things go wrong. It's great that we don't know everything. It allows us to make discoveries.

If instead we paper over our discomfort with blame, it leads to scapegoating. We blame either an individual or a whole community, simply because we need an event to have a human cause to feel in control.

Blame seeks to slice groups of people down the middle and put them in one of two categories: victim or perpetrator. It divides rather than unites. It isn't interested in solving problems or taking positive actions, only the hollow victory of victimhood or the agitation of anger. Anger is a bright and powerful flame that can be useful to initiate change, but it burns out fast. It's like driving your car in first gear only – it wrecks the engine. You can use anger to get things started, to fight against genuine injustice, but staying angry obscures, rather than illuminating a better way ahead.

Making a mistake versus being a mistake

The third and most damaging of all the blame beliefs is this final one, where we confuse someone f**king up with them being a f**k-up. I talked about this earlier in relation to our own self-care.

Say, for example, you order coffee, and the waitress, while pouring your drink, spills it on your laptop. If you're worried about the consequences of your computer possibly breaking, you slip into blame instead of just thinking 'They spilt coffee', you may also make the judgement that they are clumsy or bad at their job. If you are feeling particularly fearful, you may label them 'useless'. I say fearful because these judgements are simply a bid to try and avoid feeling your own fear. If your laptop is ruined, what next? Will you get into trouble at work? Will it cost a lot of money? Can you afford it? Will the waitress help you pay for it? You're not actually angry, you're afraid. And so you condemn her, saying that this coffee spilling is a sign that she is worth less than you.

Angry blame is often fuelled by fear. When someone is angry at you, when they are on the attack, see if you can hear the fear underneath it and what that fear needs. Then speak to that, rather than allowing the anger to hijack the conversation and direct your response. It's really easy to meet anger with anger, but this doesn't solve anything. Remember, blame is simply a reflection of someone's emotional state – it's not an accurate assessment of the situation and you do not have to take it as such.

You do not have to tolerate people shouting or blaming you for things that aren't your fault. You can walk away or you can ask to be spoken to quietly. However, under some circumstances and if you feel able, you may want to try the tactic of treating the anger as fear. Imagine that the person full of resentment is simply telling you that they are scared. Keep calm, find out what they are afraid of and soothe that fear first. It might be easier to find a solution.

Along with generating anger and negativity on both sides, the 'blame' way of thinking rebounds negatively on our own self-worth. If an action with an undesirable outcome means something undesirable about the author of that event, it follows that we ourselves are not allowed to make mistakes without labelling ourselves as mistakes. Forget that as toddlers we learn to walk by falling over or learn about what is dangerous by hurting ourselves.

This incredibly self-restricting belief means that if we misjudge our own actions, we'll be forced either to go into denial when we f★★k up, condemning us to continually repeat our patterns, or to hide in the shame cave (more on that next). It's just not true – making a mistake doesn't mean you are a mistake. You are more than what you do.

SHAME

If blame is a bridge-troll, shame is its toxic cave-troll of a sibling. Shame lives in darkness and silence, alone, in the place where love goes to die, a frozen landscape.

Shame, like blame, is a defensive tool, and similarly one that, despite seeking to protect us from feeling pain or discomfort, often ends up causing more damage than whatever caused it in the first place. It's perhaps even more hurtful than blame, although it's a branch of self-blame, because it pollutes our entire world. Blame disconnects us from one person or group of people who we think is wrong. Shame seeks to convince us not that we did something wrong, but that we *are* somehow wrong as human beings; and what's so awful about this conclusion is that we can't escape ourselves.

When we are afraid there is something wrong with us, we pre-emptively isolate and disconnect to avoid being rejected. We falsely believe that there is nothing we can do to change the situation – that the fundamental fault lies in our being. We hide our actions, parts of our characters, feelings or experiences that we falsely believe are ugly, broken or deformed, from everyone – even those close to us. Brené Brown says, 'If you put shame in a Petri dish, it needs three things to grow exponentially: secrecy, silence and judgment.'[17]

Shame's love of isolation makes it dangerous – it means we cannot get the support we need to deal with whatever it is that caused the shame in the first place. Sharing and being heard is immensely healing. Shame is not really an emotion, but a frozen layer of ice hiding the hurt or whatever unacceptable emotion or attribute we feel is underneath it. In shrouding what we think lives under that shame – either from other people or even ourselves – we are really hiding those parts of ourselves that most need attention and care. It is like going to the doctor's for a check-up and chatting about a sniffle you have, but failing to tell him about a massive bullet wound in your back and hoping he doesn't notice.

There are some people that think shame is useful for

keeping our behaviour in line, for stopping society from running ragged, for making us good people. I don't agree. There is a lot of shame in this world. If it really worked like that, we wouldn't have the problems we do. Shame doesn't stop problems, it just stops us from getting help. Worse still, those suffering with very high levels of shame won't seek help until total annihilation is on the horizon. Anyone on a self-destructive path doesn't just sabotage their own life, they impact on others as they spiral downwards. We are all deeply connected as humans, perhaps more than we realize. Whenever we reject or disconnect from someone, there are two or more people that get hurt – the one pushing away and the one pushed away.

Shame, because it makes us assume people hate us, is highly destructive. It's associated with eating disorders, social phobias, addictions, anger and rage. We don't feel able to talk about our experiences, and we feel unable to correct them – after all, we are the problem. This leaves a lot of emotional energy nowhere to go, and many people suffering with shame will channel it into toxic behaviour, all the while anticipating that the same fault that caused the initial undesired behaviour will bring around failure again.

Shame makes us so darkly inward-staring we don't even realize that there are other people in shame's cave with us, in the exact same situation, feeling the exact same thing. Shame is so deeply preoccupying it makes it hard for us to empathize with others – it makes us forget we are human, that we are fallible, that frankly, we are made to f★★k up. We're so busy focusing on how wrong we are as individuals, we can't see all the other mitigating factors that influenced the situation, or other people that might have played a part. We assume we are omnipotently wrong.

It is empathy, in the end, that saves us from shame. Where shame makes us believe we are different, recognizing our humanity helps us realize we are the same. If we can talk to others about our experiences, and be listened to with kindness and acceptance, we begin to remove that freezing layer from our souls so we can actually feel the grief or fear or pain, express it and then look at what needs to be done to move forward.

One major fact that must truly be felt if anyone is to recover from shame is that just because we take part in some hurtful behaviour, we are wrong. It doesn't define us permanently: it's not our true nature. This doesn't stop us from taking responsibility for our actions – far from it. It is shame itself that prevents us from being accountable, because we've been wrongly assuming that we are somehow uniquely flawed, with an abscess on our character we can't remove, rather than that we simply made a mistake. When we unhitch what we do or have done from who we are or can be, we are given some space to breathe. We can express remorse, and look at ways to mend or clean up the messes we have made, and over time, and with support, trust in our own worthiness and ability to handle the situation in the future. We can take the right levels of responsibility without crumbling into self-loathing and hiding away in isolation.

This idea that we are not defined by our actions may be a struggle for some to swallow. We love labels in our society – if we steal, we are a thief; if someone says something nasty, they must be a fully-fledged bully; if we betray someone, we are a love rat; if we say a sexist thing, we must be a sexist. Then we infuse all these labels with so much pungent revulsion that it's almost as if being called one writes us off as humans for life. People make mistakes. We are undeniably more than what we do. Our value can't be defined by our job, our salary, how many marathons we run, how many cities we've visited, how many people fancy us or how many kids we have.

Your life is not a series of doings but a journey of becoming. You may learn how to become through doing, but it's not a straight road. You actually need to do it wrong if you want to get it right. Mistakes are how you learn. F★★k up or you're totally f★★ked. Don't you just love this spiritual stuff?

Coming out of the shame cave

Think of an experience you feel some shame over. Call it into your mind, and breathe into your belly. Be soft with yourself. Remind yourself: 'I am a fallible human, my value is no less or no more than anyone else's.' Now it is time to melt the ice, express what you feel and tell the situation as it is. You can write it down, record a selfie video, or if both of these feel too much, put your headphones in, play some loud music and say it out loud, either somewhere private or in front of a mirror. After you've done this, ask yourself, 'How might this be not just about me?'

HONESTY

Hiding from honesty is the quickest route to loneliness I know. An unwillingness to say or hear what's real and life becomes devoid of intimacy. Lying about your feelings is the emotional equivalent of shutting a door in someone's face. Both sides lose out on a chance for genuine connection, and the only relationship you have is one with your own fantastical perception.

That doesn't mean being truthful or hearing someone express honest emotion is easy, feels comfortable or looks good. The reward for honesty might be love and connection, but arriving in that place is a process requiring humility, practice and a few f★★k-ups. It requires trust in the power of vulnerability over self-doubt, worry, imperfection and rejection. Honesty is a dialogue and its main aim is intimacy; it is not, as some would have it, about causing offence as you walk away from someone, blaming the other for being too sensitive while crying 'it's a free country'.

The intention of honest communication is important. It is not sharing controversial opinions for no reason other than the joy of broadcasting or feeling your impact – that's attention-seeking entitlement. Honesty is not an excuse to offload your unprocessed emotional gunk onto other people, simply because you have a mouth, phone or a keyboard and you can. It requires you to take responsibility for your feelings even while you share them: they are your emotions and opinions and ultimately their onus is on you to handle them. It asks you to speak not only truthfully but in such a way that people can hear your communication – phrasing yourself so that your meaning isn't masked by provocation or unnecessary upset. If that requires you to step back for a minute and find out how to say what it is you need to, then so be it. It does not always need to be impulsive.

So often, truth-telling isn't seen as something that may allow us to get closer if we stick around and seek understanding, but is instead treated as a dangerous weapon, a kind of emotion-laden medieval mace, wielded about in times of trouble. It feels so threatening we only use it when there's nothing to lose, when the time has passed for amends to be made successfully. We only really tell our boss the issues we faced at work during the exit interview. We finally share with our partner all those things that annoyed us and what we really wanted during sex, as we break up.

Sometimes, we hang on to our truth for fear or shame, and only release it when we've totally lost control – say in an argument – but often our honesty becomes so smothered in blame, bile and defensiveness that any nugget of authenticity gets lost. Then we end up apologizing for what we said and discounting it, though it's actually just the delivery that was off.

Other times we smuggle truth into an angry confrontation because, although our souls demand that we say it, we don't know how to find the space and we are nervous about how it will be received. We are being sneaky. We know in a row it's less likely to be heard – that emotions are so high, it will just get lost in the melee of sensation. We pretend to ourselves we are giving honesty without truly imparting it.

Honesty is not a weapon, it's a catalyst. Sure, it can be volatile. But just as fire can be destructive, in the right hands it can also be purifying. Honesty puts the heat of our attention onto a particular situation, emotion or issue. This heat has the capacity to change the shape of whatever it comes into contact with. Humans naturally fear change, but that doesn't mean it's always bad. Just as glassblowers work with molten glass under intense temperatures, or goldsmiths plunge the gold into the hottest part of the fire in order to mould it, honesty provides the heat to alchemize our relationships from base elements into something beautiful.

The honesty cycle

At its core, honesty is pure love. It asks us to reach into our hearts and attend to what's there with all the humility and grace we can muster. We will see parts of ourselves we want to hide from and uncover feelings we'd prefer not to feel. Yet honesty demands we move towards these heart-cracks like valiant mountaineers. This is the first stage: being truthful with ourselves.

The second stage is living in accordance with these truths, attending to what is there and sharing the pain and fear and hurt as well as the happiness, desire and longing with the humans around us. To be honest with another about what lives in our hearts is to take on terror – to face down the fear of loss, abandonment, rejection, rage. It means sacrificing fantasy and risking reality – choosing the anarchic electricity of life over the comfort of sunny, syrupy romance. It does not always need to be the bad stuff either – honesty is as much happy loving truths as the ones that might be perceived negatively. Remember, though – not everyone wants honesty. If you feel that might be case, ask if someone is willing to hear and respect their reply. This is not about violating people with 'your truth'.

The third stage of this honesty cycle is being willing to hear another person's honesty, to listen and receive the truth with an open heart. Hearing honesty can be as hard as being honest, but it is necessary – it helps us to practise love and acceptance – both for ourselves and others. Often our reaction to others' honesty takes us back into our own selves where we can uncover more truths about our character. Practising this honesty cycle with those we love refines and polishes our character, bringing our dark and light sides into play, generating self-knowledge, acceptance and intimacy.

Yet honesty is so taboo that we don't often get to experience this – instead, we mollify and pacify, sharing only the palatable half and burying the important part. Or we simply lie.

Mostly this is due to fear, shame, lack of trust or disrespect. However, we convince ourselves it's because we don't want to make anyone uncomfortable or be socially inappropriate. We don't only lie to ourselves and others; we lie to ourselves and others about why we lie to ourselves and others.

Remember, there's a difference between harm and hurt

– harm is pointless and destructive. Hurt is inevitable and recoverable and can lead to growth and reconciliation. It hurts when you have an operation – even if that operation goes on to save your life. Honesty can cause hurt – but it shouldn't cause harm.

Demonize or patronize? What you're choosing to do when you lie

Language is already layers on top of experience. Even when we aim to tell the truth, misunderstandings happen.

When you know what feels honest for you and instead you choose another route – silence, half-truth or deception – you dishonour yourself, your relationship and the other person.

Why are you lying? Perhaps there's an assumption that the other person can't handle your honesty – that your truth would be too much, or they would not be strong enough to handle it. Either way, you're demonizing yourself or patronizing someone else. Underneath that, you feed a belief you'll be rejected if you truly share who you are or what you think.

It's not true. Sure, from time to time some people will find honesty hard to handle. Tell the truth and some may temporarily or permanently disconnect from you. Not everyone, though. And far fewer than you might imagine. People respect honesty and strong relationships do survive. The only way you discover this is by putting it to the test.

Lying is cruel for two other reasons. The first is that by constantly only telling half the truth of your emotional reality you lose touch with your own feelings – you hide yourself from someone else, only to buy into your own lie. How are you treating yourself if even your own emotions aren't allowed?

Another unkind side effect of lying is that if someone senses that something is going on for you and asks, only for you to lie and pretend everything is fine, then you are contributing to them thinking their perception is off too. People instinctively know what's true – when you don't tell them, they either think they are going mad or assume the truth is something much worse, which is why you don't want to share it. Your lies can infect someone else's reality.

But what about those people who seemingly don't want to hear an uncomfortable truth? I myself have struggled more than once to receive some, ahem, perceived criticism, even while recognizing the courage it would have taken, as a friend, to share it with me. If you want to be honest with someone but you are concerned it could have an impact on their feelings, or it might be hard for them to hear it, ask yourself these four questions first:

1. **Do they already know?**
   If you believe your friend or partner is already aware of the reality, then you may want to offer your love, support and a space to talk, rather than simply imparting facts, or letting them know that you've also noticed, which is likely to just make them feel worse. For example, if you're concerned about a change in a friend's behaviour, be that eating,

drinking, working or going out, they will very likely be aware of the changes themselves and that they are masking a deeper problem. Simply saying, 'We think you are eating/ drinking/partying/working/shouting too much' is unlikely to be received well. It's up to them whether they choose to accept help or not.

2. **Why are you telling them?**

There is only one reason that flies here – to build a deeper, more connected relationship. Discharging a load of so-called honesty (whether it's true or not) to make yourself feel better or put them in their place is not going to build intimacy, because it's a personal attack for selfish reasons – a game that only has one winner. We all get angry and honest sometimes and it's not the end of the world or even your relationship if this happens, but it might not be the best way to communicate your concerns.

3. **How are you telling them?**

If this is a particularly emotionally charged topic for you, it might be a good idea to remove all blame from it first. Write down what you want to say or scribble out all your emotions on a piece of paper first. One time when I was leaving a job, I wanted to tell the truth but I didn't want it to come out of my mouth in a string of angry venom, so I wrote my own run-through resignation letter first, so I could leave without resentment.

4. **Ask them**

If you've checked in with each of these questions and believe your motives are good, it's okay to prepare your friend/family member/co-worker with some words that allow them to tell you whether they want to receive your honesty or not. For example, 'There's something I want to tell you, but it's hard for me to say and it might be hard for you to hear – would it be okay if I told you now?' You could also offer to text them later or tell them over the phone.

Little lies and lying by omission

Some people think telling white lies is acceptable – that small amounts of dishonesty in certain situations is, in fact, far more moral than ruthless honesty. Some people think that by leaving certain facts out they aren't lying – even though the takeaway from the situation is significantly altered.

There's a good argument to be made in favour of kindness – and sparing someone's feelings when they aren't seeking truth but merely reassurance or approval. Sometimes we ask, 'Does my butt look big in this?' when really we mean, 'I don't feel attractive today – can you help me feel confident?' Or we ask, 'Do you like the meal I made?' when we really mean, 'I hope you can feel my love – can you?' We aren't perfect beings and if you can hear the more truthful request behind the words themselves, you might want to answer that instead.

Sometimes, however, asking for honest feedback when you just want to be acknowledged or praised is a hard habit to break – and it's usually broken when you repeatedly get what you ask for and it feels bad. I know this one – I used to send friends copies of articles I'd written and ask: 'What do you think of this?' when I really wanted to hear what they liked about it, what they agreed with in it and to feel good that they had read my piece. I soon realized, after I received some genuine warts-and-all feedback, that genuine feedback was definitely not what I was after. Now, if I just want praise, I ask specifically what people like about it. Fundamentally, though, what someone else thinks – honest opinion or not – is never more important than our own sense of worth.

The question of whether to tell the truth or not depends on intention. If you are holding back some information from someone, despite honesty benefiting neither them nor your connection in the long run, then you are scared of the small demands on your honesty for the same reason you shiver at the big challenges. It's best to be flexible around this: you don't need to whack someone with a bunch of honesty if they're already struggling at the end of a long day – it's going to be hard for them to hear you then.

Being truthful in small places, even when it's uncomfortable, can help us build the communication skills necessary for those big moments of honesty. It allows us to practise being assertive. It reveals how strong both we and our relationships are; that we can experience disagreement and the overcoming of small conflicts and criticism ('I hate it when you put the couch cushions on the floor' or 'I really don't like that thing you do in bed' might be one example) and survive anyway. I also think that when we engage in white lies or hold back a key truth, we miss out on those moments of unconditional love. We forget that we don't have to like everything about each other to still fundamentally trust, love and enjoy connecting with someone else.

Lying recap

Think of the last time you told a lie – or failed to really share the truth about what you thought or felt. Why did you do that? What was the belief about yourself, the other person, or your relationship that made you do it? Ask yourself if continuing to act in line with that belief is beneficial or painful to you. What is the impact of acting like this on those around you?

BEING UNCONDITIONAL

Every year, millions of people stand tremulously in front of friends and family and promise to love their partners 'for better, for worse, for richer, for poorer, in sickness and in health … till death us do part'.

This thirteen-word promise, written into Christian marriage rites, is a simple ideal of unconditionality that for many of us is at the heart of what we believe about love.

Yet being unconditional is alien to our everyday lives – we might glimpse this kind of love with a pet or with a child, but most of us have lost touch with how to be unconditional in the way we express ourselves with others. For all the hundreds of thousands of people who get married in the UK

every year, around half that number also get divorced. (Office
of National Statistics). Marriage is a hard practice, and unless
we are specifically religious, we're not offered much in the
way of guidance or example. But even God has conditions for
entry to heaven, right?

Living in such a highly transactional culture, being
unconditional has become a kind of mystical moonshine, a
beautiful concept but inaccessible to the earth dweller – too
far from our lived experience. There is nothing inherently
wrong with being transactional; conditional exchange, some
argue, is a foundational element of society, established to
manage and limit any inclination to act in ways that serve
ourselves best.

Political philosopher Thomas Hobbes argued that the
natural state of man was a state of 'war'; and we need social
structures, which rely on law, the rights of property and
fair exchange. Without these, our lives would be, as Hobbes
famously quipped, 'solitary, poor, nasty, brutish and short'.[18]
We might wrinkle our noses at his cynicism, but we still lock
our doors at night, we still check our change as we exit the
supermarket. Essentially, putting conditions on things works
very well in some areas of our society – for the legal system,
in shops, for mortgages.

However, living without some level of unconditionality in
relationships – being unable or unwilling to give or receive
unconditionally from others – is a slow death for our souls.
It's also practically impossible, not to mention exhausting,
continually totting up what we owe or are owed by those

closest to us. If we keep constant tally of who last bought the milk or took the bins out, how can we remember who loved first last time, who allowed themselves to be vulnerable first, or who forgave first?

This is life, too

'Unconditional' literally means without conditions: without qualifying, or providing a caveat. It means completely and totally committing your assets, be they your time, your trust, or the investment of emotional energy, trusting that these gifts won't be appreciated or returned.

It is saying 'yes *and*' rather than 'yes *but*' (that's a trick for people who love going to improvisation classes there). It allows, accepts and embraces rather than restricts, disputes and grips. When it comes to love, it's the warm, pink marshmallow cloud we all want to bathe in, first from our parents, if we're lucky, then from our spouse and then, perhaps, from our children.

If I aim to be unconditional in how I relate to my life, this means accepting, enjoying and being grateful for everything that comes into my experience, whether I want it or I don't. It's a conscious choice to enjoy life whatever the circumstances – not just based on the 'right' conditions (which, ironically, do not exist anyway). It's a contract with myself to seek pleasure and appreciation even in the most unlikely places, or adverse situations.

It means asking myself, 'How can I enjoy this?' when the train is packed on the way to work and there's sweat dripping down the back of my new shirt. (It's hot, I feel alive, I'm grateful for my body working to cool me down.)

This embrace of life means that when my date cancels, and I'm all dressed up with nowhere to go, I'm willing to ask, 'How I can turn this around?' (Seeing what friends are around to meet, noticing that I am disappointed but it's not the end of the world, taking photos of myself looking pretty.) It means knowing that delicious juice can be squeezed from the ugliest fruit – and not ignoring, resisting or rejecting the parts of life that, just for me personally, are harder to appreciate. It's an attitude that is constantly reminding me 'this is life, too' – that rain and storms are just as much part of existence as warmth and sunshine.

Learning to welcome and appreciate both as equally necessary is our job, providing the balance and variety that makes life both challenging and beautiful.

Being unconditional with myself means adopting this practice at an even deeper level. From birth, many of us have learnt (largely unconsciously) to divide ourselves into two: good and bad, acceptable and unacceptable, successful and unsuccessful, lovable and unlovable.

While these demarcations might be useful for functioning in society (it might be 'good' not to steal something, or to espouse racist views, for example), it's not a great way to relate to yourself.

Underneath these labels, I seek to embrace all sides and parts of me. I choose to love myself whatever – if I fail, if I get fat, if I f★★k up – I won't reject myself. It is what it is, life is now, and I will not put conditions on my happiness or love for myself.

That's challenging for most people and confronting for many. We tend to think flagellation results in positive change – if we beat ourselves up enough about our bodies, our work, our faults, we'll be magically motivated to lose weight, gain muscle, earn millions, and be generous.

We also think we prefer people who are modest, who play themselves low, or say they know nothing. A note on 'humility' here. Humility is not insecurity or inadequacy or repeatedly resolving to do better, or putting down what we do have. Humility is actually the ability to listen better, to hear what's true and what's just noise or fear. It's the ability to see better, rather than looking through a lens that only allows you to see what is good in you and what is bad in others. Perhaps you wear the other set of contact lenses – the ones where you see only what is bad in you, and what is good in others. Humility allows us to see both, simultaneously, and make lots of Venn diagrams. It helps us to notice what we share with other human beings, even the ones we may initially dislike. That's one reason humility is such wonderful friends with unconditional love. Because it is concerned with what is, not what we would prefer, it allows you to stop focusing on the future for a minute and to see what's here right now.

Many of us today have very narrow ideas about who we need to be and what our life should look like before we're allowed to accept and enjoy it. That we need to be a certain weight or age to wear a certain dress, or speak a certain way to be on the radio. Perhaps we need to have a certain level of intelligence before we are qualified to write a book or be on TV; that only with a certain amount of a certain experience are we allowed to offer advice or opinions. It is a very common belief today that we need to have a specific amount of money or number of university degrees to qualify for the label 'successful'. Yet as a result of all these limitations on us as we try to live our 'best life', we eventually feel antagonized when people who don't fit these arbitrary standards seem carefree, happy enough to wear the tight dress, write the book, start the podcast and say they have a successful life.

Then, even when we hit the benchmark, we move the goalposts, so we never actually get the reward of the self-love we needed and promised ourselves we would feel when we started. Those places you don't want to love are actually the bits that need it most. If we approached food the way we treat our relationship to self-love, we'd only let ourselves eat when we weren't hungry, or have a sip of water when our thirst was quenched. It's nonsense. Love yourself anyway.

Cultivating a full and loving heart is very helpful when it comes to practising unconditionality in relationships. Relating to people is hard; it's one of the most important components of our happiness and we're not taught in any structured way how to do it. In all relationships, you'll need to accept and love yourself along the way, in all those places you are still conditional, transactional and consumptive. One side effect of practising being unconditional with yourself is that you naturally begin to generate a softer position towards others, realizing that most of the time, we are all doing the best we can, and we have more in common than we think.

All sounds too good to be true, right? Okay, so here's the catch. Life is conditional and humans are conditional: we all need food, water and a whole host of other things to continue to survive. That's the challenge: how can we be unconditional in these very conditional bodies?

And what does that mean when it comes to relationships, which, as we all know, usually come with conditions too (we might call them standards, or expectations – I prefer to call them boundaries, because they are there to keep us safe, not measure how we're falling short), too. There are two ways of being unconditional that I'll discuss here: giving and receiving. Each are two sides of the same coin, but there are slightly different challenges with each. But first: what being unconditional in relationships does *not* mean.

Being unconditional does not mean you give everything you have, even when you don't want to, just because you feel you should. This is people-pleasing, and it's a one-way ticket to resentment. Being unconditional does not mean you put up with things you dislike all the time or that hurt you. That's abandoning yourself and having poor boundaries. Being unconditional does not mean demanding everything another person has and expecting them to give it to you. This kind of behaviour reflects an attitude of entitlement and it's a sure-fire way to make sure you're never satisfied.

Whenever we give or receive unconditionally, we create something that is of far more value than whatever service or object we are providing or accepting. From one heart to another, a little light stream of love is ignited. A connection that is based on abundance, gratitude and compassion.

It does not depend on conditions being met, neither can the conditions be unmet, and so the beam cannot be broken. This cycle of loving reciprocity spools endlessly, a kind of revitalizing, regenerative energy. It is the kind of energy to endeavour to develop in a relationship with yourself, with life and in your relationships with others.

Try this: think of a place or a time where you felt restless, itchy or dissatisfied. What conditions were you putting on that moment? Sit quietly now and call it into memory. Try breathing in acceptance, love and letting go of expectations as you exhale. You could also try softly saying to yourself the mantra: 'I expect nothing and appreciate everything.'

GIVING

You're probably familiar with the golden rule: 'Do unto others as you would have them do unto you.' It's a maxim that appears across many different cultures and religions, including the ancient civilizations of India, Greece, Rome and Persia; and is one of the main principles of Christian ethics (forming the bedrock of the teachings implicit in Jesus' Sermon on the Mount).

Unfortunately, this tenet has suffered a slight semantic shift over the past two thousand years; one which changes the meaning entirely. For many of us, our relationship to giving has mutated from one that begins from a place of humility and love, to one tied to expectation and demand: 'Do unto others, so that they do unto you.' A lot of us will only give to get, rather than giving for its own sake.

We pick up the phone and listen to our friend moan about their parents for ten minutes, so that we can moan about our parents for ten minutes afterwards. When someone thanks us for helping them, we reply, 'You would do the same for me' – a phrase that can sound more like a threat than a compliment.

In a business meeting we might promise, 'You scratch my back and I'll scratch yours.'

After work, we meet someone for a first date and buy them dinner. We offer to pay. If they let us foot the bill, we'll be asking ourselves up for coffee. That's how it works, right? The ones who refuse our money usually don't call back.

The relationship's good – until we say 'I love you' and they don't respond in kind. Outrageous. How could one person love someone more than the other?! That would be insufferable. Unbearable. We demand fair amounts of love to be exchanged at all times. After all, we only give Christmas gifts to the people who treat us in return. And Secret Santa has a budget for a reason. Fairness is crucial.

Aside from this transactional *quid pro quo* approach to giving, we also frequently put conditions on our 'gifts'. Maybe we only give to people who we judge are deserving, people that we consider have the 'right' to receive gifts from us. For example, we might not give our sympathy to the rich man who suffers from poor mental health because 'life is still easier for him'. We won't give our money to a homeless person because 'they would only spend it on drugs'.

These are examples of conditional giving: when we will only give if the recipient seems worthy, or we offer on the basis that we receive something in return. We can do it consciously, knowing we definitely want something in return and we will be resentful if that thing doesn't come. Or we sometimes do it hopefully – we don't necessarily know if we will get anything in return, but that is our primary motivation: for example, if we act with generosity because we want to be liked or to look good. If we're Christian, perhaps we give because we want to get into heaven.

All of these conditional ways of giving, while understandable, limit us and the potential for our future relationships.

One of the reasons for this is that our choices in giving are often driven by a fear of lack; that there is not enough to go around and our stores will not replenish themselves.

It is difficult to acknowledge the flaw in the assumption that there is no joy in giving for giving's sake, that people will not help us unless they can expect something in return of equal or more value. It feeds into a worldview where we are only worth what we are able to give – only loved or valued for our skills, services, money or possessions.

So, we instinctively cling on to our resources, and spend our lives on the lookout for thieves or freeloaders, simultaneously trying to acquire more and more. If we buy into this philosophy, it means we ourselves don't ask for help because we feel as though we are a burden if we're unable to give anything in return. It means we don't trust people who give to us, because we are constantly waiting for the day of debt to arrive. We're forever forced to say sorry instead of thank you. This perspective is deeply limiting, sentencing us to a depressing, mercenary existence.

Guilt costs more than you think

There are other kinds of conditional giving at work in our lives, too. One occurs when we give not to get something back, but because if we don't we feel bad. We give to negate the shame of choosing not to help. We do it even when we don't want to do it, and often with resentment (this gift's emotional 'price tag'), because we feel we have to – we feel it is 'owed' by us. We help our friend move house even though we'd rather sleep in, or we go to our sister's graduation even though we find it boring and pointless. We give our neighbour a lift to the airport at 1.00 a.m. through gritted teeth; we may not like them that much, but we do it because it's expected and we'll feel guilty if we don't.

Dutiful or guilty giving is our way of avoiding the discomfort of learning how to give unconditionally. We give, even though we didn't want to, and we convince ourselves this faux selflessness is enough to make us good people. In my mind, though, this giving is still transactional – we give to clear our consciences, or to avoid being seen as miserly or selfish.

I believe this kind of giving is the most toxic, because we

disguise it as altruism, as being unconditional, but it hinders us in developing true generosity.

Giving on this basis often allows resentment to take root and fester within us; a resentment that we blame on the other person for asking. We then do the task mindlessly, ignoring the rising rancour (although this is often sensed by the receiver) instead of questioning our own feelings of scarcity or setting up a boundary to give only what we feel we can willingly, without resentment or expectation. It's fundamentally untruthful to the other person, and to ourselves, and stops us from ever experiencing the joy and freedom of unconditional giving.

Practising unconditional giving is not about giving away everything you have. It's not about letting people take from you, or being obliged to say yes to everything. It's about knowing what you are comfortable to give without expecting anything in return. Of course, you might get a sense of warmth and strength and love for yourself and the receiver, but then again you might not.

Setting your terms

Establishing what feels acceptable in giving is hard for us to do initially. Start small. For example, say your friend wanted you to come and help her pack up to move house over the weekend. It's your first weekend off for a while, and you want to be helpful, you know it will be fun for an hour, but you don't want to give up your entire Saturday and Sunday for free. You have a few options. You could lie, and say you aren't around that weekend. The benefit of that is that it's easy to make something up and you don't run the risk of hurting your friend's feelings or feeling guilty. The cost, of course, is that you are lying, your friend might sense it and you have to remember not to give yourself away while you upload that lazing-in-the-garden-with-a-spritzer selfie (#metime #sunnyafternoon #blessed) to Facebook. You could instead say yes, try and make the weekend fun, and remember she owes you one for when you move house. Perhaps you plump for an alternative option. You can either tell her you can do one hour at a certain time, as you want to relax that weekend, or you could stretch yourself a little and say you're around for two hours but you get to choose the playlist for the second hour.

There is something I have realized about myself: there is no price high enough to do anything that I can't make fun. I don't care about duty, obligation, shoulds, money – whatever I get in return. If it isn't fun, I don't enjoy it and I can't make it so, then frankly life just feels too short, and it's time for me to say no. Sometimes this isn't even conscious – the universe just magically creates conditions that mean it is impossible for me to show up. I'm late, I forget, or I end up overbooking and having to cancel. This has happened so often I've decided to stop trying to make myself do things I never felt like doing in the first place.

Letting go of crutches and clutter
Giving unconditionally, for me, is fun. I find it both hugely freeing, and revealing. In trying to give unconditionally you

get to see what you are attached to, what biases or behaviours you have adopted, your crutches, your clutter, the situations where you are scared to let go. However, it can be truly liberating to live this way. When you give unconditionally, you are telling yourself and everyone else, 'I have a full, bountiful life, with no shortages; I have so much that I am willing to give things freely, with no expectation of anything in return. I am enough and I have enough. I am secure, I am safe. I trust.'

The secret that not everyone knows (we're too busy guarding our hoards and trying to snaffle what we can for free) is that giving actually makes you feel good. We are actually biologically built that way, because we evolved as cooperative animals, living in groups to survive. Professor Matthew D. Lieberman puts it best in his excellent book, *Social*:[19]

Mammalian brains are wired to care for others and among primates this caring extends to at least some non kin, even when there is no material return on the investment. Because of the way our brains are wired eating a piece of delicious cake is enjoyable whether we are hungry or not. Similarly, helping others feels good whether we expect something in return or not.

It may take some deep inner work, but at some point there will come a time when it doesn't feel like giving any more, at least not giving in the same sense as you once understood it. Your love, attention, compassion and care, your time, even your physical belongings or your money – the very act of giving them unconditionally reaps even more wealth. This kind of giving generates compassion, trust and love. Think of the famed Buddhist image of the candle: even in relighting a thousand more candles, the life of the candle is not shortened.

Choosing to share your light and warmth are gifts from an infinite source; the choice to give unconditionally is the gift you give yourself and others at the same time. It also takes courage, to say no and be true to yourself as you start, so that you can say yes to more and more in the long run.

Try and give a little bit more and more unconditionally. The best way to do this is in gradual increments that don't threaten your conditioned sense of fairness immediately; see if you can stretch yourself.

RECEIVING

Receiving, for many, feels deeply uncomfortable, whether accepting physical gifts, compliments, attention or even love. The archetype of the receiver is not valued in many societies; instead, self-sufficiency is lauded and help is derided as a 'handout' and the receiver demonized as a 'scrounger'. It is seen as more powerful and soul-worthy to give than to receive. We operate this way, largely forgetting that for someone to give, there has to be someone receiving.

Nonetheless, we struggle on, trying to bargain our way through intimacy, believing everything must be paid back – if not financially, with physical objects, or our time, then emotionally, with effusive gratitude and ego-boosting compliments. Even in sex, if we receive pleasure, we feel we must return the 'favour'. Those times when we can't avoid receiving, then we devalue the gifts of others or simply try to rebuff them. 'Oh, you like this dress on me? It's so old and look I'm bursting out of it at the back. I actually think it's pretty ugly.' This is the emotional equivalent of taking someone's Christmas present and, just as it touches your hands, crushing it, spitting on it and tossing it back to them.

One of the teachers at the organization where I did my coaching programme, used to call this habit 'discount jeans', based on our tendency to say 'Oh, these jeans? I got them on sale' when we receive a compliment. We minimize the gift because receiving makes us vulnerable. Receiving can feel so destabilizing that often we panic in our inability to receive graciously and feel intensely awkward. Our egos demand we maintain a social image of plenty, of self-sufficiency; thus, bizarrely, a degree of wounded pride can be the consequence of a loving gift.

Sorry, Mum and Dad

Receiving requires humbly confronting the limits of what you can do or want to do and appreciating the existence of another and what they can offer. It means accepting graciously without resenting that you need their help (I'd just like to take this opportunity here to apologize to my parents, who have definitely had some resentment thrown their way because of my own insecurities). It sometimes means acknowledging that someone was able to provide something for you that you didn't even realize you wanted, need or would appreciate until it arrived.

The popular notion of giving and receiving sees the first as active and the latter as passive – and somehow that has come to mean submissive and less potent. However, the internal process of receiving unconditionally requires a huge shift of consciousness and a great inner strength and sense of self. It's just as active as giving, but in an invisible, felt way. It's not the same as simply getting, demanding or taking. Receiving graciously requires us to actually open our hearts.

In receiving unconditionally, you make a declaration. You are telling both yourself and the giver: 'I am consciously allowing you to provide for me something I could not do or get, did not want to do or get or did not think about doing or getting for myself.'

Everyone has something to offer

Unconditional receiving asks us to confront our own conditioning and judgement, too. It means not qualifying who you will accept from or what form their love takes. It means knowing that as a teacher you can receive something of immense value from your student, even though they may have studied less. That the CEO can receive valuable insight from the man on the shop floor. It's believing, until it becomes knowing, that everyone has something to offer that is worth receiving, and it is important that we value and honour this by accepting it graciously. Is a few pounds from a poor man worth less than thousands from a billionaire? Allowing people to willingly give or serve is a statement of their value. Rejecting someone's unconditional offer because you perceive them or what they have to offer as less than you is ugly and narrow-minded. Sometimes accepting gifts can be hard, though, especially if the empath in us understands the kindness or self-sacrifice required to give the gift relative to the giver's situation. Could you accept change for the bus from someone who was homeless, willingly given, even if you needed the money to get home?

Occasionally, we put conditions on receiving because we think there is not enough, as in the example above. At other times, we are afraid to fully receive, because what is being given feels so good, bringing us a deep sense of warmth, gratification and pleasure. We worry that, if we let in the good stuff, we are also opening ourselves up to experience pain when it ends. It's almost destabilizing. It's a bit like those times when you don't feel able to relax into your holiday because you know it's going to be over soon, even though below that fear you are craving to enjoy how great it feels in the moment. It's safer to refuse.

This vulnerability is amplified when we are receiving unconditionally. We feel that if we didn't 'earn' it, it could definitely be taken away from us. That if we don't deserve it, we might have to give something away later to someone who angrily demands something to redress the balance.

We occasionally tip over into entitlement to try and avoid

feeling these things, coming up with reasons why we deserve things to calm our anxious minds. Or we reject the gift altogether. It's crazy – we are so afraid of coping with change that we'd rather stay miserable than face a dynamic reality. If you had nothing and then you had something and then it changed and you have nothing again, you haven't really lost anything per se; you have just gained an experience.

We might try and block receiving, but we are receiving all the time. Believing you exist on a solitary plane where you are not constantly receiving is wilful denial or a failure to see reality. Yet it's understandable. When we truly realize how much we have received, it's overwhelming. What have we done to deserve it? Well, maybe a few things, but we're still enormously in the red, and by that token there is nothing we can or could ever do to deserve all these gifts.

It's a false comparison. Your life, love, relationships and value can't be processed like a bank balance. We're not talking about houses or clothes or holidays any more. We're talking about human experiences, which simply can't be tallied in notes or numbers. Life is not about earning or deserving, it's about experiencing and becoming. The way you 'pay it back' (it's really more of a case of honouring) is by fully receiving it: acknowledging it, experiencing it, leaning into the gift and the joy of it and taking pleasure in it.

Here's an experiment for you: try becoming a person who takes so much pleasure in receiving that you are a joy to give to. So often we scrunch our noses and crumple our shoulders awkwardly when we are given something, wracked with guilt and worried we don't deserve it. This ruins the experience for the giver as well. There's actually something beautiful in receiving even though we haven't earned it. It means people are giving you things because they *want* to give them to you. Because they love, respect and admire you and it's fun for them to treat you. In 'keeping score' or employing a tit-for-tat mentality, you fail to recognize the message with the gift: you are loved. That ought to feel good.

Giving, receiving and redressing the balance

Sometimes I think we should all just be a bit more dog. A happy dog doesn't care what it is that's being given – anything from a pat to a bone is brilliant – and it doesn't care why, or who's giving it. It is simply joyful for the connection.

This is how we receive unconditionally: by accepting graciously something we haven't necessarily 'earned' and enjoying it fully, because it's just so wonderful to be offered a gift in this way. By choosing to receive like this, we enable unconditional giving. Receiving unconditionally, we become part of something beautiful, an endless feedback loop of abundance and love. And by treating ourselves in this way we realize we are beautiful and valuable no matter what we do. We didn't actually have to do anything to deserve it; we just had to be.

Receiving in this way is challenging, and it doesn't happen overnight. Plus, there are practical issues that arise – for example, if you want to receive something unconditionally, but you suspect someone else is giving it with strings attached.

Of course, their strings are their responsibility (especially without a frank conversation; we aren't telepathic), but you still may feel awkward.

What if someone else gives me something and expects something in return? First things first, remember the strings are attached to the giver not the receiver – they are their strings. So in one sense, that's not your problem.

However, there's also a slightly softer way of handling it: Juliette Karaman-van Schaardenburg, an empowerment coach, says, 'If I feel the offer has strings attached, and my hesitation in accepting usually means there are some, I ask and it usually opens us up to much more connection and intimacy.' You might say something like, 'I'd love to receive this but I'm sensing there might be strings attached – is there anything you are expecting in return?' After all, you might be comfortable with the strings. It's nice to be kind here, too; remember that none of us is perfect – in our receiving or our giving.

What if I don't want the thing being offered? Think about why you don't want it. Is there no use for it? Is it going to impact negatively on you in some way (e.g. your home is too small for it, etc. etc.). Will it make you feel uncomfortable? If so, a simple 'No, thank you, but I really appreciate the gesture' will suffice, and remind you that you are allowed to protect your boundaries. Another option, if they really want to give you something, is to tell them what they could give you instead:

'Perhaps rather than going to the cinema we could take a walk and have a chat instead?'

What will happen if someone wants to give me something and I don't think they have enough? It's not your job to worry about that. It's your job to receive fully and with grace.

What if I want to give someone something unconditionally and they want to give me something in return for it? Well, you can tell them it's not necessary but, hey, why not just receive it gratefully? Someone is trying to give you a gift – enjoy it! Life is good!

SEX

I'm not always thrilled about having a feeling body as my home. Not only does it involve those tricksy little wastrels called emotions; it also means being constantly interrupted by pressing physical demands (e.g. sleep – food – water – headache), which, paradoxically, I often find completely interfere with life. However, the big mother in the sky gave us a large compensation for living in a warm fleshy vibrational greatcoat, and that, in my opinion, is good sex.

Good sex, or, for the sake of this section, the experience of pleasurable intimate physical connection between two or more consenting adults, is, for me and many others, one of the fundamental benefits of being alive. It usually involves genitals, but it doesn't have to: ideally, you want your whole body and whole self involved. It definitely doesn't have to involve penetration or climax. Good sexual connection makes me feel healthier and improves my mood. There have been a number of studies into the benefits of regular sex, including stress relief, lower blood pressure and improved immunity.[20]

Sounds great. So why aren't we all doing it more? Well the good news is it's nothing to do with our sexual attractiveness or genital/digital dexterity, it has everything to do with fear, shame and conditioning (three of the strongest antidotes to pleasure, you'll ever find). I'm writing about sex from my perspective of being a woman with a vagina, but even if that's not you, hopefully, this section will help you view sexual connection from a fresh perspective, inspire you to get more in touch with your sexuality, and maybe even try a few things at home.

Sexuality: aka glorious chaos

Sex can be one of the most dynamic and beautiful ways to enjoy being embodied in connection with another human being. Trouble is, it affects us so powerfully sometimes that we can find it destabilizing. Sexual energy is one of the few forces that can judder us out of numbness and into feeling, and not just feeling, but feeling in connection. If we're not used to that, it can make us feel vulnerable and it can also bring to light things we usually ignore or aren't conscious of. This might look like fear: that we aren't good enough, or we're too much to handle, or that we will be abandoned. It might look like cultural conditioning ('If I have sex with her she'll want a relationship, right?'). It might even be a surprising kink, or something that we find pleasurable but are also a bit embarrassed by. Sexual energy blows everything out of the closet. It leads to greater self-discovery and, in the long term, freedom – but it can be very confronting. As well as showing the best of us, it also shows us the dark and primal side of our mind and our nature. Burying these feelings doesn't make them go away, it just gives them more power. Pouring light, love and self-acceptance, as well as a genuine curiosity, can help. Remember, humanity is thousands of years old. There's nothing that you find sexually confronting that hasn't already been dealt with or experienced by many others.

Sometimes, because sex illuminates in this way, we assume it is dangerous, when really it's just a mirror powerful enough to show us what is going on in ourselves. Forget hips; it's genitals that won't lie: if they want it, they want it, and if we aren't feeling it in any way – maybe we don't feel safe or can't get our mind off a work project – well, they aren't getting off. You can't control pleasure and attraction, so of course religion, science and culture have been cautious and clinical about it. Plus, sex makes everyone feel vulnerable. We need to talk and be open-minded with each other about it so that we have a chance at experiencing the kind of transformative pleasure, intimacy and connection that sex can offer us. Face our fears without the jokes, the bawdiness and the put-downs, the self-deprecation, the silly names for our genitals or the jibes at the opposite sex. Without shaming others or censoring ourselves. Without focusing on 'performance' or 'pleasing your partner'. First, we need to unravel a lot of our sexual conditioning, though.

Let's talk about 'shoulds', maybe?

Ah. sexual conditioning. A system of beliefs intended to protect us from getting hurt, but which instead have kept us all so disconnected and scared of each other that we end up wounded anyway. You know the ones – the ones that got twisted somewhere and gave us words like 'sluts', 'players', 'f★★k boys', 'creeps'.

This menagerie of myths can lead us into saying 'yes' when we mean 'no' and 'no' when we want to say 'yes'. We say 'yes' to the man who seems like good relationship material, who has the good job and the stable future, even though inside our body we feel nothing. We say 'no' to the man who's uglier than us, who's a bit fatter and laughs too loudly, even though there's something about him that is so sexy. We shut down the impulse when we're attracted to someone of the same sex and pretend it's merely admiration, when our genitals know otherwise. We decide to settle down because we think we ought to or because we actually like someone.

The list of 'rules' we've been taught about sex and relationships is long and wonderfully general. Here are a few you might have. Recognize any?

- *Men always want sex and/or only want sex.*
- *Men use women for sex.*

- *Women deny men sex to punish and control them.*
- *If a romantic partner/date does something for me, I must reward them with sex.*
- *Withholding sex is a good way to get into a relationship.*
- *You shouldn't have to wait longer than a month of dating before you have sex with someone.*
- *If you have sex with someone right away they won't respect you.*
- *We can only have sex if we want a relationship.*
- *Only people who are objectively of the same attractiveness should have sex.*
- *Women who have sex with you quickly are easy and sluts.*
- *Men who want sex or fancy lots of people are creeps.*
- *Sex without penetration isn't sex.*
- *Men need to ejaculate to have a good time.*
- *You must know how to please your partner and always bring them to orgasm.*
- *If I am not good in bed or always available I am a bad partner.*

None of these statements is true in any sense that's useful. Men do not always want sex; just like women, they get tired, stressed or don't feel sexy. The human need for affection and partnership isn't gendered. We've all 'used' sex at one time or another – for physical relief, as distraction, for thrills, as a 'reward', or to avoid actual intimacy. Doesn't make it right, or even particularly effective for what we're using it for, but it doesn't mean we do it all the time or that it's a specific gender problem. Just because a woman sleeps with you quickly, doesn't mean she's sleeping with everyone quickly; also, why do you care? You don't own her. There's not a specific time-frame by which you should have sex or not, in any relationship. No quotas. This is merely insecurity unloading itself as judgement. If you're only going to have sex with people you're in a relationship with, or going to be in a relationship with, you're either going to end up not having a lot of sex or end up being in relationships with people you don't really like. Similarly, men are not creeps just because they have a large sexual appetite and don't know how to express themselves well. That's a big ole label you've stuck on them because you feel uncomfortable with their attention and saying no. Sex without penetration is still sex. Some of the most intense sexual experiences to be had are *sans* penetration. If you don't believe it, try it. Only twenty per cent of women climax through vaginal penetration. Think outside the box. Expand your mind and expand your pleasure. It's not all about climax, but about connection and intensity. Sex ends when one person has had enough. And 'had enough' doesn't mean when they have orgasmed and it doesn't mean it's not been great; it's just sometimes, the moment passes.

When we buy into these beliefs wholesale, we get our hearts and genitals all wrapped up, feeling fairy tales that aren't true. We block physical intimacy, heaping a whole load of meaning and stories on sex that are so far from the simple truth: two people enjoying intimate physical connection.

Sex means nothing more than the act itself. That's it. When you have sex, that is all you sign up for: a little space of connection. I'm using words like 'nothing more' and 'that's all', but actually sex in this way is pretty special. It doesn't need an overlay of cultural conditioning – or fear and possessiveness – to try to make it something it isn't. I believe sex can be more sacred when we do it for its own sake, rather than wrapping it up in power dynamics and game playing, ultimatums and 'must-haves'. We don't need all the symbolism and covert significance – it's beautiful as it is.

It's hard to feel only this, though, about sex – there are always things that are going to creep in; old fears that will pop up and need attending to, and little beliefs that are still present: that maybe he should stay the night if he respects you, for example. It's good to investigate and stay true to what yours are before you create any type of passionate connection, because often we aren't aware of them, or we assume everyone shares our beliefs, and then we get hurt when these uncommunicated personal conditions aren't honoured.

There's a lot of talk about foreplay, but a lot of us forget to discuss after-sex before sex, which I think is just as important, if not more. How we like to be held, and how long we want body contact to continue in that afterglow. If we want them to stay over. If this means we are now 'serious'. What does honouring your connection look like to you? Do they check in with you in the following days to see how you are? Do you agree to meet again afterwards? Are you now exclusive? To avoid feeling too vulnerable after sex, here are three questions to consider asking yourself before it:

1. *Do you want to be intimate with this person right now?*
2. *Do you know what you need to feel safe: emotionally and physically; before, during and after?*
3. *Can you communicate this and can you trust it will be listened to?*

Trust is a funny one when it comes to sex. One of the reasons we can have such amazing experiences with each other during sex is because we are embodied humans, but it's the very same thing that makes us so fallible – and both ourselves and our partners unpredictable emotionally. The most we can ever do is learn how to trust in ourselves, know our own value and trust that we will be able to cope with whatever curveballs are thrown; maybe our partner doesn't reply to our calls after sex, and we can learn from that experience; what happened there, and what we could do to help ourselves next time.

Good sex gets us out of our heads and overthinking everything, and into our bodies, where we 'experience'. When we do this, quite often those feelings are so strong and so pleasurable, they manage, indeed require us, to do the thing that we resist doing in all other areas of our life – surrender to the sensation and the moment. Utterly blissful and also pretty terrifying – it can feel disorientating and vulnerable to come back to earth and we can get all sorts of wires crossed.

Sometimes we get confused and mistake surrendering to

the moment and the sensation in our bodies for surrendering ourselves to another human being. That can make partnerships needlessly strained – one person feels scared, as if they've handed themselves over and now need their partner to take full responsibility for them, and the other feels daunted by that challenge. Really all that's happened is we've had an intensely pleasurable experience of letting go. It doesn't mean *not asking* for what you want to feel connected, whether that's cuddles or pillow-talk, but it does mean not handing over total power for your welfare to your partner.

Another place we risk handing our power away is when we outsource responsibility for our sexual pleasure to our partner. Good sex requires *you* to know what you like and be able to ask for it. It also needs you to know what you don't like and how to communicate that. Your pleasure is your own responsibility. It is not up to your partner to know exactly how to please you. Of course, it might be preferable if your partner is willing to listen and get a little curious themselves; and maybe you could be willing to listen to them in return, mix their desires with yours and get a little curious, too, but it's not your or their obligation or job to know what either of you wants without communicating it. So often, either we don't know what we like or we won't ask for it. This means we'll just let them keep rubbing the wrong bits, label them bad in bed, all the while not giving them any chance to make it right. Maybe we tell ourselves, 'This is just as good as sex gets for me.'

There is a well-used myth: *that orgasms are given.* The truth is, no one 'gave' you anything or 'did' anything to you – those feelings are yours and you own them. They happened in your body – no one handed them to you and no one can take them away. You show up ready to have an orgasm, and it naturally happens. It's not your fault if your partner is not getting off, and it sure as hell is not your trophy if they are. And vice versa.

And then there is the other way we don't take responsibility: when we outsource our emotional response to our partner. If they say no to sex, we think they're no good and they're in the wrong. The truth is, your feelings around this 'no' are yours to take care of; your sensitivity to rejection. Maybe your partner just has a preference for no sex right now?

Experiment with making a list of what works for you, then divide that list into the following:

- *Turn-on triggers: Things that turn you on straight away, even if you weren't thinking of sex already or aren't in the mood – this can include things people say, how they act or what they do.*
- *Pleasure menu: Things that turn you on during sex or physical connection – places you like to be touched and how you like them touched.*
- *Turn-offs: Things that really slow you down or that have to be adjusted before you can be in the moment and enjoy sex.*

Putting this 'list' into practice, if anything doesn't feel good during sex, slow down and gently talk, tell each other what floats your boat. If there are times when you are just not available sexually – tell them. This is particularly useful if you have a long-term partner – know when you just don't want sex so that you can tell them 'There are times when if you instigate sex with me, I am more likely to say no.' It might be late on a 'school night', maybe you have your period, or you just aren't in the mood. Stand by your feelings, and don't confuse 'no' and 'yes'.

Knowing what your turn-off triggers are can be just as helpful as knowing what turns you on. Three that often strangle libido are expectation, worry and lack of safety.

Expectation is a massive passion killer. For example, if I think I am being expected to do something – whether that's climax myself or make my partner climax – then it feels much less fun; like a task, rather than an experience. If that's you, then it's a good idea to set a time boundary – say, for example, that you touch for half an hour, rather than aim for climax, which may or may not arrive. There's some logic here, too – orgasms are a bit like sleep in that the more you try and force them, the less likely they are to come. Unwanted expectation can hang around the notion that physical intimacy has to include genitals or breasts. Stroking arms or kissing necks can be just as intimate. Embrace the feeling you have in your whole body more, rather than simply making love and paying attention to the 'sexy' parts. The back of the knee, the ankles and the inside of the wrist can also be potential and underappreciated erogenous zones. The one thing that corrupts sex the most is that we can't just experience touch for what it is. No one, while stroking a cat, suddenly turns round and tells the cat, 'My turn. I've stroked for twenty minutes now.' It's just understood that stroking in and of itself is a pleasurable experience for both. However, in sex, we have a tendency to get very obligated and transactional – and only by breaking this mind-set can we see what we are doing.

Worry and lack of safety make sense as turn-offs. When a woman orgasms, the vigilance centre in her brain – the part that keeps her safe – switches off. So a woman needs to be able to relax to climax. The thing is, your worries, your feeling unsafe, are not anybody's responsibility to provide, even your partner's. You can ask for things that help, though. These might be a commitment to hold you afterwards, to go slow, or to reassure you that if you change your mind at any point, they will stop. (They should anyway, but it can often be comforting to communicate this again.)

Design your own sex life

I believe that humans can develop the emotional maturity, communication skills and internal safety to have good sex outside of a committed, monogamous relationship without abandoning their higher selves. It's all about intention, responsibility and willingness.

Your sexual connections can look however you want them to, but in my opinion it's preferable to have an intention that honours you both as adults indulging in pleasure together, rather than using each other for relief. Take casual sex seriously. Have an intention (like being in the moment) that honours you both. Say what you want and what you don't want. Be willing to listen and be willing to f★★k it up.

The journey to good sex involves a lot of less-than-good sex. That's okay. It doesn't mean anything other than this sex was not as pleasurable – it doesn't make the person a bad lover or person; it doesn't mean there's something wrong with you. At the end of the day it's all just sensation. If you can learn something from it, great! If not, then just relax and allow the next time to roll on by.

COMMUNITY

There's an African proverb, 'It takes a village to raise a child.' Essentially, it means that one human needs an entire community of people to help them grow into an adult (I think it also means it takes a village to support the mum and dad, too). But nappy rash and sleepless nights aside, this proverb also applies to anyone who wants to step into their full potential, to access the generous, loving, talented, calm and creative human being that lives inside us all.

It might seem appealing, even glamorous, to forge ahead in the world solo: autonomous and wholly self-sufficient. Lord knows, I've thought of myself as a lone wolf more than once; lone wolves are known for being stronger, more aggressive and more dangerous. The image of this solitary beast in the snow battling the odds for survival is seductive to anyone who has had to face challenges to get ahead; whether it's fixing the photocopier, struggling to pay the rent independently or navigating a difficult emotional situation. If you're ambitious, talented and want to make a change, it can be surprisingly easy to get hypnotized by your own power and vow to do it on your own.

The thing about lone wolves in the wild, however, is that they can only hunt small prey or scavenge. To take down bigger animals, wolves need to hunt in packs. Very few lone wolves remain on their own indefinitely – almost all wolves join another pack, despite being rejected by their initial group.[21]

What we can learn from the lone wolf analogy is that it is not wise to hunt solo forever. Success is more likely to come for you through cooperation and shared aims. There is a great quote by Zig Ziglar: 'You can have everything in life you want, if you will just help others get what they want.'[22]

A pack of wolves is stronger because its strength relies on its component wolves – or 'two heads are better than one' – so, just from nature, we can observe that the need to belong, to be part of a community, is a primal one. In my experience, the best way to value community, and its power, is to join or create one. It is the most nourishing way to expand into the person you are fully capable of being and achieve all the amazing things you can accomplish. This section is going to explore how to get the most out of the communities you're already a de facto member of (work, sports teams, family) as well as the ones you might discover, and even, if you dare, create yourself.

I've been calling it a community. You could call it a tribe

(that's trendy right now), a gang (though traditionally this has negative connotations), an 'order' (also got a bit of baggage), a company, a team, a group, a collective (quite nineteenth century), a congregation, a sorority, a fraternity, a club, a cult (if you're starting a cult, make sure it's friendly and you may want to avoid talking about or serving Kool-Aid), a union, an association, or if it gets really big … a movement. There are a lot of words for humans in groups, perhaps because we're deeply social creatures, naturally inclined towards cooperation. What I mean, loosely, when I reference community, is a group of people with something in common – a shared interest, shared values or needs, a shared location, a shared identity or a shared cause. Emotional connections form between group members and everyone is (for better or worse) involved in some way – contributing and benefiting from the existence of the group as a whole.

Knowing that you can rely on and trust in a group shields you from the unnecessary worry a lone wolf endures; if you don't know how to solve a problem, you can feel secure that there will always be people available for support – that even if you are not particularly close to them, they will help you in a time of need, not because they are choosing to be charitable, or because they will get something back from you, but because of your shared bond.

Communities provide individuals with the courage to take risks towards their goals, grabbing opportunities which otherwise they may have felt too insecure to take alone; with the sounding board and support of a community, that leap into the unknown seems less dangerous. Feeling the backing of a community, and knowing that if you fail, there will be someone from your community waiting with a trampoline, ready to bounce you back up again, provides an incredible sense of freedom in and of itself, but community provides a lot more than that. It feeds one of our primal needs: that of belonging.

American psychologist Abraham Maslow[23] proposed – in his 1943 paper 'A theory of human motivation' – a hierarchy of needs that all humans have. It was arranged in a pyramid, with physiological needs at the bottom (food, water, rest, warmth). Safety needs next. And third, sandwiched in the middle of the pyramid, is belongingness and love needs.

Being part of a group provides a vital sense of belonging. When we are in a community, we experience acceptance – we are welcomed by others and feel valued as part of a group. It is vital to have a sense of our own intrinsic value separate from this, but being part of a community can also reflect our own worth back to us as we contribute to it, and help us on that journey towards finding ourselves, our worth, our strengths and our unique gifts as individuals. This may quieten an anxious striving within us, a fear that drives us on; desperation to achieve simply because if we don't, we aren't valuable. Being part of a community with a shared bond sends the message that we are worthy because we are like and liked by others – that we are enough. This leaves us free to achieve what we want to do, instead of pushing aggressively for accomplishment because our worth depends on it. Striving for acceptance from the community only devalues our sense of self, as opposed to the ideal situation, which is where outside approval complements our sense of intrinsic value and bolsters a positive self-image.

Above 'Belonging' on Maslow's pyramid, comes Esteem, Prestige and Accomplishment, and at the top, Self-actualization – achieving one's full potential, including creative activities. Belonging might sit in the middle, but 'community' can help provide *all* of the needs on the pyramid. Community security, leading to personal freedom, is the type of cooperation and sharing that provides you with a huge amount of knowledge, motivation and meaning.

Knowing how you interact in a group is invaluable in teaching you how you communicate and what types of roles you gravitate towards playing, and those you avoid. They can give you a chance to practise leading – as well as what makes a good worker or supportive deputy. Whether you like to rebel or make yourself invisible. It's great to notice yourself doing these things and ask yourself why. Noticing these natural inclinations, and questioning *why* you feel them, can help you to uncover more about yourself: are there potential roles you could be playing but haven't had the confidence to embrace yet? Playing just one role in a community restricts you and stops you from relating to others, as well as preventing you from suggesting improvements that benefit the community as a whole.

Listening is great, but if all you can do is listen, whatever inner analysis and problem-solving you may be doing will go unheeded and make no contribution to the collective. Similarly, leading is a wonderful skill, but if you can only lead, you'll always be dependent on people being willing to follow. Being able to take on a whole kaleidoscope of roles, a talent we learn in community, gives you more freedom to act in a way that best suits any given situation we come across in life and allows you to empathize with others in similar roles. Don't hate on the driver until you've been one, basically.

Just through being part of a number of large online conversations with multiple participants at any given time, I've noticed how I like to take part in community in a number of different ways: how I like to rush in to take care of people with a problem. Even if that means I feel uncomfortable about voicing opinions against those of the majority, or that I worry I'm talking too much or being ignored. Community is the glue that keeps us together when we want to disconnect or isolate ourselves — and those places are valuable for teaching us about ourselves and how we relate to others: how we can move through conflict instead of just abandoning ship when things become trying.

Growth

If you're doing community right, it will frisk you right to your very bones. Although communities pull together because they have a shared cause, interest or bond, not everyone, to use a phrase employed by a particularly snobbish politician I once interviewed, will always belong to the group of 'people like us'.

You are probably going to be thrown together with some difficult characters: bossy ones, ignorant ones, people who think toilet humour is funny when you don't, those you consider snooty and pretentious, highly offensive people who offend easily, sock-and-sandal wearers who think it's acceptable to comment on your fashion sense, etc., etc.

You may have consciously chosen this community (say by joining a sports/arts club, choir, women's institute, fundraising committee) or unconsciously found yourself with them (moved to a new area, put into a team at work, family). Either way, they present you with a challenge.

Entering (or being thrown) into a new group of people is always the moment all your insecurities, the chips on your shoulder, and your worst social anxieties start vying for dominance of the floor. A dance troupe of your personal demons that otherwise no one gets to see. Contributing to a community can be tortuous on our egos but it illuminates all our private self-deceptions. Yes, communities can, and very often do, bring out the worst in us. From those snide initial snap judgements we make on other members (hopefully in our heads), to posturing for dominance, or shrinking from visibility. All these behaviours are automated reactions based on our desire to establish a foothold, find our role in the group, feel secure, validated and useful. As awful as these struggles sound, this is actually good news, because once you can see and feel these behaviours at work, you can change them for something more constructive.

I've been a member of a number of different communities

in my time, from meditation groups to flat-shares to work projects (and let's not forget extended family Christmases). Every time, I swagger in with some idea that I'm a fully actualized, emotionally mature, spiritually aligned adult with excellent communication skills. Every time, I'm stomach-churningly humbled to discover I have more to learn. When I'm working as part of a group, my insecurities resurface – I sometimes find myself holding back and not contributing because, though I could help, I'm afraid what I have to offer won't be good enough and I'll be embarrassed.

Then there's another side of me that emerges – my superiority complex, which is challenged by the community itself. I might find myself thinking, 'I'm so much better than this person, I don't need them.' Other times my patience is stretched ('Lord, it would be so much quicker if I just did it myself'). Then there are those fears of scarcity – that there isn't enough, I won't get enough and I don't have enough; although if I'm honest, those appear every time my table orders a sharing platter at a restaurant (my friend scoffs all the best bits of bread while I'm in the bathroom).

Contribute, cooperate, create

One of the reasons communities are challenging is because they require you to contribute – quite often in front of a group of people. Although you may have a shared bond with these people, you largely don't know them well. You might be asked to introduce yourself, tell people a little about yourself and what you can contribute to the group. This can make you feel intensely vulnerable. At first, you do it on trust alone; and although you get much out of community, according to how open and active you are willing to be, these benefits aren't always obvious overnight.

Personally, all of the above challenges my natural 'lurker' – the side of me that likes just to sit on the sidelines and watch, rather than take part. If you have lurker tendencies, too, you're not alone – the 1 per cent rule in internet culture is the general observation that in online communities only 1 per cent create the content and the other 99 per cent simply lurk. The '90–9–1' version of this rule states that for websites where users can both create and edit content, 1 per cent of people create content, 9 per cent edit or modify that content, and 90 per cent view the content without contributing. The openness required to be in community can be immensely confronting – but it also allows you to realize parts of yourself: both your generosity and your inner miser.

The openness required by community has been a great teacher for me. I refer to everything that is hideously uncomfortable and that I don't enjoy as 'a great teacher'. Try it, it's fun. Semantic tricks like this appeal to my dark sense of humour; e.g. 'That boyfriend was a great teacher for me' (he cheated on me twice).

I like to think if I at least learn from the teacher the first time, the same lesson isn't going to come back round again. Cultivating an attitude of openness is a hard lesson but has taught me to embrace and appreciate others' perspectives. This allows us to collectively create richer narratives, more welcoming dialogues and deeper, more meaningful conversations, better projects, better outcomes. Essentially, by increasing your willingness to share what you have, others are generally more likely to share more of what they have, with you. In so doing, your community pools its resources, be they material, intellectual, creative … (even emotional or spiritual in the context of support or prayer groups) to achieve its shared aims.

The growing industry of crowdfunding is a perfect example of how communities converge to harness the power of collective resources; where individuals are inspired to donate what they can to a project, brand, event, relief effort or campaign after reading about it online. Some fundraising targets can be exceeded many times over, and the joy of being able to achieve your goals from a platform built by people who may not know you at all, but care enough to share their hard-earned money with you, can be truly heart-warming. It also serves as a reminder of our intrinsic goodness, and how good it feels to give, restoring our faith in humanity when we see people who reach into their pockets to give what they can.

When you're taking part in community it's really easy to look around the table (village hall, yurt, video conference call or whatever meeting venue is used by your particular group) when something is being discussed and think, 'I don't want to share this here, these people don't deserve my knowledge/ideas/skills/time.' You might think, 'I can't be bothered … this isn't my responsibility', even though you have a shared interest with these people and a vested interest in this community succeeding. Perhaps one member of the community is being particularly vocal and irritating you – so you sit, silent and smug, safe in the knowledge you have more experience in that area and are better placed to serve up a solution. You might not want to offer your help because you see it as the group feeding off you, or you might even worry that someone may steal your ideas and claim the credit. This sort of jealous protection is bonkers, irrational and limiting. It is, however, very common, and motivated rarely by reality, but by our own fears; a toxic cocktail of inferiority with a shot of bitterness and a little superiority cherry on top. Delicious.

There are a few different ways to handle this feeling when it rears up within us – the approach I've found most rewarding, however, is to stop conceiving of myself as 'sharing' my resources, and instead plug into the idea that I'm contributing to creating something bigger. It has the effect of making me feel much more generous, focused and bound to a higher creative purpose.

It's not about 'working for free'

There's respecting your value, honouring your talents or the business you have built, and then there's jealously guarding an accumulated stash of skills, ideas and knowledge until it actually ends up impeding your growth.

Those who get grabby like this remind me of Smaug, the dragon from *The Hobbit*. Dragons famously sleep on piles of gold and attack anyone who comes close. There's mixed consensus on this, but one reason dragons do so is apparently because of their one weakness: they set everything on fire! So they can't sleep on normal bedding. Another possible reason suggested for dragons sleeping on piles of gold is that the gold embeds itself into the dragon's soft underbelly and forms an armour. We are not dragons. We are naturally cooperative creatures. We do not have the dragon's weakness. We don't need to be terrifying fire-breathing monsters guarding our gleaming hoard.

A life lived on the defensive is no life at all. It means you can't relax. Hence why dragons sleep with one eye open. If you adopt Smaug's attitude, you'll only feel peaceful when you have nothing left to protect.

I'm no monk; I don't believe having no possessions is the route to freedom or happiness. I think it's possible to be open-hearted and generous, while asking to be paid what I feel I deserve, when relevant. Community is a great place to find out where this fine line is drawn – and guess what? The lines can shift under your feet before you know it.

Teamwork makes the dream work

I went on a spirituality retreat once, and like so many of these weekends, it was astronomically expensive. As with all of these experiences, it began with the deeply sacred practice of paying vast amounts of money to be made to feel immensely uncomfortable.

I'm exaggerating. There was electricity, hot water, and we were actually cooked for. However, after our first meal in our new rudimentary accommodation, one of the course leaders stood up and started dividing the washing-up and cleaning duties between us for the weekend. I'll tell you what: the ferocity of my expression and the fire in my chest meant I felt pretty Smaug-esque at that point. I had NOT paid an extortionate fee to clean toilets and scrub dishes.

> Altruistic behaviour happens in the animal world, too. For example, humpback whales are known to rescue seals from killer whales, swimming in and dispersing the pod of killers, allowing the seal to escape.

However, there was something wonderful about the whole experience that I'm not sure I could have gained another way. The first thing was that I had to work with people to get the job done as quickly as possible, which meant I had to get on with them, and appreciate their value in helping me work. The second is that it was wonderfully levelling. I was giving my time and energy away for free but I felt more part of the experience, more connected with everyone there, more part of the whole set-up where we stayed. I felt valuable and somehow lighter: less weighed down by my own self-importance. It felt like, working together, we had created something special.

In Sikhism, they call this *seva* – or selfless service – and it's a way of getting closer to God. Sikhs are taught that inner peace and freedom comes from *seva*, a serenity that cannot be found elsewhere. Kamalpreet Badasha, a British writer in her thirties, who lives in London and was raised as a Sikh, spent Sundays at the Gurdwara with her grandmother performing *seva*: 'As a child I would help make *roti* (flatbread), serve food and wash dishes for the free communal kitchen. Only as I grew older did I realize how unique this routine was from a world perspective … *Seva* for me is a way of getting closer to that pure energy of doing something for the greater good.'

Sharing can mean growth – for you and for the community

The word 'sharing' means divide up, but I don't think that's the case when we 'share' things like our time, ideas or skills in community.

Some might say it's more like 'giving them away', but that's not quite true either. Information and insight are not pizza – you don't have fewer slices if you offer some up. What are you really giving away? No one can take your knowledge from you. Sharing your passions, thoughts or talents only reaffirms them, refines them, energizes them. Sharing in this way is a creative force – it strengthens and deepens these abilities and gifts. Were they really yours to cling on to, anyway? Most of the time we learn from or are inspired by other people. We should embrace sharing our skills, knowledge or ideas. If we should be wary of anything at all, it is not using them – or not applying them well. Unused tools get rusty; it is the same with the brilliance inside of us.

However, we get all protective, competitive and withdraw. Half the time we're so focused on thinking we have everything to lose we can't see all there is to gain. We forget that in a community, whatever we contribute to the pot is returned to us threefold, in ways we can't imagine yet. None of us can predict the future. We can never know how much we may depend on others in the years to come.

The ancient fable of 'The Lion and the Mouse' by Aesop is a perfect illustration of how our actions in the present can come back to us later in life. In the story, the lion is about to kill a mouse who has disturbed his slumber. When the mouse begs forgiveness, the lion shows mercy and lets the mouse go. When the lion is later captured by hunters, the mouse recalls his leniency, and gnaws through the ropes, freeing the lion.[24]

What the fable teaches us is that when we're the ones with the skills, we feel powerful and in demand, but there may be a time when these skills are useless in the face of an unforeseen need and we turn to someone else in the community for help. This has happened to me time and time again. Sometimes, the person I least expected to help me is the one who offers a kind smile and says something that totally throws my life into perspective on a rough day. The person I hated on my first day at work becomes my best friend.

We need each other in ways we fail to recognize. The biggest lie we tell ourselves is that we are self-sufficient. One of my friends who recently started taking antidepressants told me she was embarrassed to rely on them. 'Where's the shame in that?' I asked her. I started to list all the things we rely on: we don't know how to fix our own toilet, so we call a plumber. We rely on the council to take away our rubbish. Most of us don't know how recycling is sorted. We rely on production lines that supply supermarkets. We rely on so many things from so many people; and most of the time we don't even acknowledge it until something goes wrong. We are social animals that have dominated this planet (perhaps too effectively) because of our ability to cooperate. Self-sufficiency for its own sake is simply insecurity driving us backwards. We create best in collaboration. Things grow when we come together.

That's why one question I am guided by when at a crossroads is: 'What am I making this decision based on?' Choosing not to help the community may be a decision based on *fear* – fearing that I won't get any benefits, or that I will experience negative effects from it.

A decision based on fear is never fruitful. It restricts rather than encourages growth. The course and nature of every living thing is determined by growth. Every living thing on this planet – from plants, to animals, to humans – is designed to grow, to thrive, to *become*. Growth is the fuel for the purpose of, and the timekeeper on, life's journey. As William S. Burroughs writes in *Junky*: 'When you stop growing you start dying.'[25]

If you remove fear from the decision-making process, you begin to make choices that broaden your outlook, expanding your realm of possibility. Deciding how best to act in ways that promote growth means you fall into harmony with life. You become more open, and then, inspiring yourself and others, you begin creating. When we share knowledge or skills, we are generating more; we strengthen relationships, gain fresh perspectives, refine and cultivate our insights. Offering these gifts up to a community you are part of generates more energy, adding to the resource pool that you and your skills are also part of. This collaborative spirit allows us to cooperate, to create something bigger than oneself. It's an immensely freeing experience, to relinquish ego for a time and give yourself up to the service of a shared aim, especially on those days when we self-importantly feel everyone depends on us.

Communities are a meaningful anchor when we get carried away on a storm cloud of anxiety about our own lives, reminding us that we are not the centre of the world. It's good to be a member of different communities for this reason, to dip in and out and know that there are worlds within worlds. They can give us perspective: there is more to life than just us – and actually that's a good thing. It helps us see ourselves clearer – as whole individuals, but also as part of many 'wholes'. Think of yourself as a part of a ginormous Venn diagram, rather than a lonely circle looking in.

The games we play

This idea is expressed in James P. Carse's book *Finite and Infinite Games*.[26] He writes: 'No one can play a game alone. One cannot be human by oneself. There is no selfhood where there is no community. We do not relate to others as the persons we are; we are who we are in relating to others.'

Carse's theory is that we play (at least) two kinds of games in this world; finite ones, where the purpose is to win, and infinite ones, where the goal is to keep the game going.

Carse's book inspired me to question my motives in a different way in order to help me choose the best course of action when I'm tempted to withdraw or become begrudging. I ask myself: 'Does this decision allow everyone to win, or just me?' or 'How can I play here so everyone gets to keep playing?'

Experience the placebo effect but with people

Being part of a community requires you to contribute to the growth of the group through making available your skills, ideas, time or knowledge to enrich the spiritual and physical wealth of the whole, of which you too are a part. You open at least some of yourself and your resources to create something greater than yourself, essentially on trust. It's not possible to know for sure if your contribution will be appreciated; ideally, the most nourishing communities will cultivate an environment where such generosity is valued, though.

Similarly, you can't know if your offering will be abused or if you yourself will benefit because of this faith. My experience in my varied roles as a coach, a journalist, a social-media producer, an employee and a manager, is that if you treat people as if they were kind, capable, even powerful human beings, they usually surpass your expectations.

Assume people are assholes and they usually won't disappoint (though guess what? Assuming people are assholes is also kind of an asshole thing to do.) When you pause to examine your motives, asking yourself questions like, 'Is fearful thinking prompting me to make this decision?' and 'Am I playing for everyone to keep playing or just for one person – myself – to win?' and choose instead the courageous, confident decision that allows everyone to win, your actions are affirming a positive view of humankind, of which you are one. Aside from the fact you get to experience your own exalted humanity, you are also believing the best of others, which more often than not results in others doing the same for you. It's a phenomenon I like to call practising the placebo effect with people.

Practising the placebo effect on people means expecting them to be brilliant. It means acting on trust that they will mostly choose to do the best thing, the thing that uplifts rather than denigrates community ties, without a smidgen of doubt in their goodness. Of course, sometimes we will be disappointed. I like Abraham Lincoln's words on this: 'If you trust, you will be disappointed occasionally, but if you mistrust, you will be miserable all the time.' True, he did get shot in a theatre, so you could argue that trust didn't help him in the end, but then again he also is consistently voted one of the best presidents of the United States ever, who preserved the Union and set the wheels in motion to abolish slavery. At the end of the day, do you want to live a big life or a small life? If you want to reach your full potential, you need to care about community, which means giving a f★★k about creating, and that requires you to trust, and invest, in other humans.

The problem with building walls around our resources is that walls work both ways. We become so restricted and closed off that we also block the possibility of freely receiving. We're so busy making sure no one short-changes us that we can't see the gifts people are willing to hand us, gratis.

Some questions to ask yourself about growth in a community context:

1. First, take a moment to consider your role in a particular community you are part of. What role do you play now? Is this role the one you want? Is it best suited to your talents?
2. Now consider your community, its aims, its purpose: how do you want your community to grow?
3. What offering can you provide to contribute to this growth?

Other things to consider:
4. To see the growth you want for the community, will your role need to change? If so, how? What inspiration can you take from other members in creating a shared vision for the future?

WORK

In a village, far away, nestled on the hillside of the semi-reality where all fables, allegories and parables take place, there lived a man who was always cold. Standing out looking at the stars one night, naked and shivering, he finally decided he needed to take action over his temperature. Why not make a jumper? He spotted some wild sheep in the distance and went out to catch them.

At first he struggled, so he got a lasso. He was warmed up by the exercise but was still feeling cold. So he lassoed some more. He got so busy in this activity that sometimes he forgot he was cold. Nonetheless, he was determined, and every night he went out, rounding up more and more sheep. Soon he had a whole flock. His body ached occasionally, and most of the time he remained cold, only now he was frustrated. He thought to himself, 'The sheep were meant to make me warm. Maybe I just need more sheep.' He spent his whole life herding until finally he realized what the problem was. He'd forgotten to make a jumper.

This is what a lot of us do in our careers. We spend all our time accumulating money and power, getting bigger salaries and more responsibilities, but money and power are never what we really want. They are just ways we think we can get what we want. And we're so busy getting them, we totally lose touch with why we wanted them in the first place.

We go to work to make money, it's true. We need to feed and house and dress ourselves. But if money is your main reason for going to work, then you're short-changing yourself, either by what you're doing or by the way you're doing it.

We spend a third of our adult lives at work. We owe it to ourselves to make sure the work we do gives us more than bigger bank balances. If all your job amounts to is you exchanging your time for money, I promise you, you're getting a bad deal. I think we need three things to make our work work for us, aside from being able to pay the bills, and that is having a job that adds value, that allows us to learn something (or progress), and that gives us some sort of enjoyment.

How do I help?

You don't have to be a rocket scientist, brain surgeon or Champions League footballer to see value in your work. It's about how you relate to the work you do.

If you're a supermarket cashier who talks with customers in a way that brightens their day, then you may find your value there. If you see your role as a cleaner as being about transforming environments into nice places to live and work, so that people feel better once you've been in a space, then this might increase your sense of value, too. We all want to be appreciated at work, but we must first seek to find and appreciate this intrinsic value for ourselves, or our self-esteem ends up being at the mercy of our boss's capacity for compliments. This appreciation of our job's value must be felt viscerally. It's not something that can be dictated to you, but a personal discovery.

There's a story in Andro Donovan's excellent book

Motivate Yourself [27]. Three men are hard at work with a shovel, digging. A woman walks by, stops by the first one and asks him: 'What are you doing?'

'I'm digging a hole, stupid,' he replies.

The passer-by walks on to the next worker and asks the same question. 'What are you doing?' she asks.

'I'm constructing a wall,' the second digger tells the woman.

And so she walks on to the third digger.

'What are you doing?' she asks.

'I'm building a cathedral,' he replies.

Paid to learn

Approaching the sticky, tough parts of your job with a view that they are essentially free training is one way to ease a little tightness around the challenges we all face at work. The places where your job is driving you crazy might be the spot where you are building up the most skills. Find it hard dealing with a difficult boss? You're learning how to manage up. Have a lot of different requests coming in all the time? You're learning how to prioritize, focus your attention, and say no.

The goal is not so much to be good at your job, but to constantly have a job that allows you to get better. If you're 100 per cent easy-breezy cruise-control good at your job, then your work isn't working for you. Mistakes are progress. If you're not failing frequently then you're not playing big enough.

Enjoyment

The easiest way to make things fun is by doing things in connection with others. If you can make friends at work, your life improves immensely. However, most of us have a natural reticence towards this, preferring to keep our distance or play politics to get ahead. We might be defensive or distrusting or hold back to avoid drama.

In my experience, when you have lots of humans working together, you get drama whatever. Trying to avoid it might be admirable, but I've always preferred to assume it's coming no matter what, so I might as well build friendships to make it worth it. Connections at work can be hard, however, especially if other employees want to keep themselves to themselves, or you just don't naturally see eye to eye on things. But it's not about learning how to work with people you don't like; it's about learning how to like the people you work with. Make it a challenge – see if you can be the sort of person to bring out the best in others. Find a similarity, something you both share (and don't make it something negative – like you both hate your jobs or hate the boss), chat about non-work things – make it clear you are more than just a drone – keep searching for something you both can connect on. Bring in food, share it, say hello and goodbye, and always offer to get the teas. Don't sit with your headphones on all day; invite people to go for a walk at lunchtime. Recognize people's talents, no matter how small. Be generous with your knowledge and time. There's always an opening for connection, even if it's the day the printer breaks. Be ready.

When it's still rubbish

That said, there are always parts of our job we enjoy less. Maybe it's the admin, the form filling or the email management. It's boring, teaches us nothing, and is perfunctory, despite requiring our concentration. I've found a 90/10 rule works for me. As long as 90 per cent of my job is doing the things I enjoy, where I'm learning, creating and adding value, then I will put up with the other 10 per cent. When it creeps over that line, I start to feel resentful, and the rest of my job suffers, too.

What about if what you enjoy is at a much lower percentage? Well, you can reframe it – looking for the value or challenge there. You can find a way to make it fun, or you can ask for it to be changed.

Sometimes, no amount of emotional levity can make the parts of your job you don't like easier and you may want to ask management if you can change something. When something or someone is giving you grief at work, it can feel like an albatross hanging round your neck – especially if you've been struggling with it for some time and can't see how to make things better. The good news is, if you've tried to change something once and it didn't work, that doesn't mean the change will never happen. It simply means the way you tried to change it last time didn't work. So now you have more 'data' – and next time, you'll want to try a different way and see if that works. The problem is not you and it's not what you want; it's just that the way you're trying to get it isn't effective. So many people find themselves facing an obstacle at work and make one or two similar attempts to surmount it; then, when they can't, assume it's impossible. It's madness. I think of them as standing facing a door you have to pull to open, and repeatedly pushing it; then, when that fails, trying to use force to break it down, and then when that doesn't work, claiming the door is broken, or it's impossible to get through, or that they don't have the skills to open it. They do, it's just they haven't worked out they need to pull it to get to the other side yet. Try something different. Patience and creativity are your allies; use them.

Culture clash

Sometimes communities promote certain values that clash with our own. It might be company principles you disagree with, or perhaps you feel at odds with the whole industry.

You might feel disappointed when you discover this conflict and feel that you should immediately leave. You might feel pressured into compliance. Hang tight. Healthy communities can thrive on dissent – it's actually not a matter of right or wrong (though you may feel it is) – and such conflict can be great for knowledge, growth and creativity – both for the community and for yourself.

First things first: don't get on your moral high horse. Values are immensely personal; they vary even within families. Even our own values change over time, and in different contexts. It's why people say things like: 'You get more right/left wing as you get older.' Or, perhaps, you might lose your enthusiasm for clubbing or hot pants.

Values are a bit like principles in that they are brilliant for providing a strong backbone and can keep us motivated when we're tempted to go off the rails, but without some flexibility, they can become constrictive. Watch those who say: 'I am intensely principled' without further qualification. In reality, what they almost certainly mean is: 'Do not disagree with me; I am incredibly rigid.'

Cooperation in community requires flexibility – it doesn't necessarily mean compromising your authenticity, but it may mean putting yourself in someone else's shoes, so you can find out what and why the other person is thinking or acting as they are. Think inquisitively rather than defensively. Understanding before advancement.

Value clashes can be incredibly fruitful if approached correctly and can lead to beneficial culture change. But even if they don't, they are useful personally. First, acknowledge you've got a strong enough sense of yourself to distinguish between yourself and the collective, which is positive. It's very easy to lose a sense of selfhood in community or abandon yourself while attempting to be part of something bigger, so experiencing this clash is actually a healthy sign. Plus, sometimes we can come to use that sensation of conflict or dislike that arises inside of us when a value is expressed that we don't like (say, someone cheats or tells a white lie to get ahead and make a sale), to show us what we do like – that we really value honesty, or fairness, for example. When your personal values come up against the collective, it's a great opportunity for growth, primarily because you will need to take some form of action – while doing so will be uncomfortable, not doing so, or just going along with it, is likely to feel extremely stressful, too.

How to approach a culture clash

This is where you need to get curious. See if you can find out why the person/organization you're clashing with thinks the way they do. This is about gathering information so you can understand and put your case forward better. Why does your boss want you to be available on email after work? Maybe she values devotion to the job? Is this her value, or is it company policy? If you can persuade her that setting tight boundaries between work and home allows you to be more present and effective at work when you're there, that this is actually a sign of your commitment and that the quality of attention you can give is more valuable when it's fully engaged, then you have a greater chance of being understood and being able to switch off after hours, without having to change workplaces.

Additionally, perhaps, there might be something for you to learn.

> There are many strange jobs in the world and one of them is definitely a 'snake milker'. These people extract snake venom from poisonous snakes like cobras and sell it to hospitals or laboratories for anti-venom. They are often employed by zoos or serpentariums and can make up to $2,500 a month.

When I was working for the BBC, I was initially incredibly frustrated by the bureaucracy and the huge number of approvals from manager upon manager that needed to be sought in order to get something done. There was a level at which it was not useful. However, there were also times when it was. My value of being creative first and foremost was clashing with their value of accuracy and reputation. Many frustrated conversations and one big mistake later, I realized those rules were there in order to protect me. The BBC was held in such high regard, was so trusted, that any errors were seen as sacrilegious by both audiences and other media alike. Getting it wrong wasn't worth the short-term creative gain. They were risk-averse for a reason.

You can also find common ground. If you're working for a company, it's likely there are some things you have in common, so that is the first place to start – where your interests overlap. You might disagree on the how, but you both are aligned with the what (the success of the company, a good working environment), so that is something worth acknowledging as a base.

Finding out what they value, seeing how what you want fits within those, and using their language to spell that out, helps. For example, the BBC has a number of core values, including creativity and trust, as well as to inform, educate and entertain. If I show how risk is necessary as part of being creative, then it is likely managers will be more willing to listen to my 'out there' ideas. Because I know they value their reputation, I might tap into that value to show how my creative (but risky) ideas could increase trust with audiences. Perhaps I frame the change I want to bring in in an audience-centric way. For example, to experiment with social media to reach more licence-fee payers in a way that is natural to them. I focus on what they will gain from taking risks, and how these things are in line with their values.

It's important to frame your argument as visionary rather than in negative terms. I've never had success asking for something by talking about bad things. People want to be heroes, not accused of being bad managers. For example, saying I want an extra member of staff because the tasks we are meant to perform are failing without it would go down like a lead balloon. I have been much more effective in getting management on side when I have explained the positive effects of giving me a certain thing. In my experience, people prefer being associated with a successful outcome than with preventing or stopping a negative one. Go to a manager with a situation where you suggest things are already failing and they clam up immediately, because it's seen as an attack. However, if you explain how a project manager will bring in incredible results, setting an example to the rest of the company about the best way to run a department, then you make the prospect of hiring one seem much more exciting. We'd all rather be seen as the architect of some great success, rather than someone sweeping up muck.

Of course, there may be times when the gap between company culture and your personal values are insurmountable.

When that happens, it's time to leave, with as little resentment as possible. Leaving a community is always hard – but know that communities are made up of individuals and quitting a job doesn't mean you have to dissolve all the personal ties you've made. They are independent of the whole. While community – and the identity we find within it – can provide us with meaning and value, it is not the only way we are worthy. Losing or leaving your job does not mean a loss of identity, though it can feel that way. No one can take away your skills or what you learnt in that role, even if the job itself is no longer part of your life.

Knowing when to quit is as valuable as knowing when to stay. Gripping on to something that makes us miserable isn't a good message to send to our souls, no matter how much time or effort we've previously invested in making it work. Quitting something that doesn't serve us is simply making space for something better. Where you work and what you work as has to work for you, too, or you're selling yourself short.

Get in touch with what works for you at work, or not, by asking yourself these questions;

1. *How does my job contribute to making other people's lives better/easier/more fulfilling?*
2. *How could I make it so that it does?*
3. *What would be the impact if I don't do my job well?*

4. *What do I find hard in this job?*
   (This is what this job is teaching you.)
5. *What do I know I am learning here?*
6. *What do I enjoy in my job?*
7. *What would be some ways to enjoy my job more?*
8. *Who would I like to connect with at work?*
9. *What percentage of things do I dislike doing or find pointless?*

You should see a picture emerging. A clearer vision of your direction. Remember, all we need to do is take the next right step and trust that the one after that will reveal itself.

SOCIAL MEDIA

Undoubtedly, social media has changed our communities; broadening them, deepening bonds, making it easier than ever to connect with others. We can now make 'friends' with someone on the other side of the world, separated by thousands of miles, our respective cultures, our lifestyles and our choices. We can (and do) fall in love through social media, and just as fast as they can be made, friendships and connections can be broken. It is one of the fastest, cheapest and most accessible ways to learn how to communicate well … and how to communicate badly.

How many times have you seen someone mortally offended in the comments section of an innocent-sounding joke? Social media reigns supreme in showcasing the full range of misunderstanding that our interactions are open to, the complexities of language and what deeply emotional creatures we are. It offers magnificent examples of the human propensity to judge and blame, puffed up with self-righteousness, and of how awful we feel when the same behaviour finds us on the receiving end.

Oh yes, it's a fantastic tool for revealing (and thus healing) your insecurities. Seeing other people's beach holiday or wedding snaps that suddenly make you feel a little wobbly in the tummy (or relationship department). It's hard to remedy flaws we can't detect, so actually noticing our fears here can be helpful, even if it does make us want to take up residence under a rock. Notice if you're jealous – and use that jealousy to acknowledge that whatever your friend's photo shows you might be something you want. Remember, everything is edited.

The first social-media platform was sixdegrees.com, founded in 1999, when you still had to scan your pictures to upload them onto your profile.

There's value in not editing yourself, though – in posting pictures of yourself that might make you feel self-conscious but once out there feel empowering. We can use social media to challenge ourselves in this way.

It's a good thing that our viewpoints on societal or political issues are also challenged online – despite talk of echo chambers, social media actually gives you access to a huge variety of different, as well as similar, views. In revealing our best and worst sides, the amount of information we can gain about ourselves by watching the way we choose to behave online is absolutely invaluable; what we hide, and share alike.

Facebook, Twitter, Instagram and YouTube, to name the big four, provide an unparalleled resource for studying the way humans interact. The rapidity and ease of forging connections on social media mean they are also a really powerful way to influence and leverage community.

This is why social media is important. Although you probably didn't log on to Facebook this morning thinking, 'Right, I've got my coffee; now I want a simple, rapid way of powerfully leveraging community', you probably will use it to talk to your friends, to see their news and hear opinions, to share your news and to entertain yourself while you are on the train or queuing for a latte, idly scanning articles or scrolling through pictures.

If you want to get the most out of social media (and hey, with all your data it's certainly getting the most out of you) it's time to look at it through fresh eyes, for a purpose other than entertainment and keeping up with friends. Online communities can teach you about people – how truly social we are – and how to stay connected without being swallowed completely by them.

Thumbs up or thumbs down?

'No man is an island,' wrote John Donne in 1624. If, nearly four hundred years ago, before England even had a postal service, John Donne recognized that as humans we were all fundamentally connected, then how much more resonant are his words now? Facebook is the second-most visited website in the world. A quarter of the world's population use it every month. It is a serious tool that enables mass communication globally. Humans are social, and one characteristic of that, as discussed, is that we build community.

> The words '**communication**' and '**community**' come from the same root in Latin – '**communis**': common or shared.

Social-media sites are a little like online Roman forums – these apps are marketplaces, coffee shops, news-stands, campaign grounds, information hubs, meeting places, and of course, dating sites. According to Facebook, there are almost five billion pieces of content shared on the site every single day. With infinite chatter, stories, pictures and ads all vying for our attention, what we then see is everyone trying to shout the loudest – and the communication at times is as savage and brutal as a gladiatorial arena.

When you log on, what you check in to is your own little select community, created partly by who you've chosen to follow or connect with, and partly curated by algorithms, which more often than not, prioritize the most engaging, popular posts.

Then, within that, there are groups of dedicated communities – for fans, for those with certain medical conditions, for dog lovers, craftspeople, people who enjoy a certain sense of humour. You name it, it's there. There are hashtags to follow on Twitter or Instagram, rules of engagement in some Facebook groups, on Reddit there's a vast and complicated etiquette – in-jokes and admins weighing in to defuse conflict, or even ban inappropriate users.

If online is community, then 'posts' are what we use to build relationships and become a valued member of the group. This may sound obvious, but there's something about voicing opinions from behind a keyboard that makes us forget that this is really just all communication between people in a community. Online we seem to forget how communication actually works, and become emotional parodies or performances of ourselves. Perhaps all that this shows is how difficult communication is in the first place.

Popularity v communication and remembering to be human

Aside from the pressure social media induces to perform 'in public', it's also used to 'self-define'. We are encouraged to self-define from the moment we first create a profile, – a 'bio' – to tell people about who we are.

When we share, we are associating ourselves with pieces of

content. Our accounts are public scrapbooks of pictures, posts and articles that we want to share with our communities – we value them, and want others to value them, (and by extension, us), too. We are really saying to our feed 'look at this (me)'. Whatever the type of content, sharing it links it with our public image. It's why crime-news articles might be read a lot on online websites, but they aren't shared a lot. If you suddenly only shared grisly murder stories, wouldn't your friends become concerned? Generally, people just don't post such things, although we all read them, unless we're railing against this kind of violence, or highlighting a misleading headline.

People largely share what they are very much for or what they are very much against. There's not much room for nuance.

One reason for this is the way we 'consume' on social media – we are usually reading on small screens on mobiles, and simply skimming. We don't have the same emotional investment we might have when reading a book. Time and attention are the stocks and shares of a very big online economy; and a lot of people are competing for that real estate. There's no time for foreplay on social media. It's all quick climax. Long, complex posts require more brainpower and, frankly, that cute dog video is just more appealing.

Essentially, we want to tell people about ourselves, in a concise, punchy, clever way, that makes us look good, and that people will read. We crave impact, more 'followers', readership, a fan base. Impact is not nuance. We know the sort of posts that elicit strong responses in us and we want ours to elicit the same responses in others. We start to post only things we believe will be popular or engage our audience. If we aren't rewarded by that little dopamine hit from a notification alerting us we've captured a little (fleeting) attention, what's the point?

Social media is great for bringing out our inner egotist. We want to look good and we want popularity. However, being popular on social media doesn't mean being liked – mostly, it means attention grabbing, engaging, whatever prompts the greatest response. Certain types of emotion are more likely to entice people to 'like' and share.

Jonah Berger, who authored a study published in *Psychological Science*, a journal of the Association for Psychological Science, found that posts that prompted a certain emotion were shared more. The aroused emotions – emotions that give us energy – like anger, fear or humour, are more likely to drive people to share information: 'If something makes you angry as opposed to sad, for example, you're more likely to share it with your family and friends because you're fired up.'

Social-media power is engaged in popularity; to be popular, all you need to do is convince people to interact with you. Unfortunately, agents of chaos, provocateurs and trolls can use this little secret to great effect. We all fall for the sensationalist/divisive posts that were designed to irritate us, to outrage us, baiting us to respond and ensure the post goes viral. It's a game, replete with psychological power-plays, ethical posturing, heavy provocation, and a lot of copy and paste. We want fame and status. If we go viral enough, maybe we could become president and ruler of the free world too?

However, this doesn't work for everyone – as online audiences become more sophisticated, so does the type of communication that holds their attention. I've learnt 'tricks' in my time as a social-media editor and producer for the BBC and the *Independent*, but ultimately, valuing 'celebrity' over a strong community of collaborators, sounding-boards and diverse viewpoints isn't a great plan. Like breakfasting on chocolate cake, it feels rich and exciting initially, but not so great when you crash soon after, nauseous from binging on garbage.

People may think they want vast armies of followers, but lots of followers don't guarantee 'engaged' audiences – trust me, I've been on the back end, watching the numbers: celebrities with millions of followers, few of whom care enough to actually read or act on the celebrity's post. Such 'stars' just don't have a strong relationship with the people in their community to really engage with them.

Conversely, there are people with a relatively small following who harness all of it and get their stories read and shared widely. Ask yourself the question – do you want people to simply recognize you, or do you want friends?

Because of the huge audiences available on social media, the strange hierarchy of verification and follower-count (as well as the way individuals with large fan bases are fetishized), it's easy to get seduced by the fame and status that social media can offer any one of us. Social media allows anyone to be 'special' once they've learnt how to 'hack' the platform – then we can bask in the illusory social power that comes with lots of followers/viewers and the constant notifications. I know one individual who simply shares a lot of missing people pictures on Twitter because it gets him retweets – and even when he knows the people have been found he doesn't take the picture down. But, what (I'm dying to ask), is the point? You have thousands of followers – but for what?

There's a great story in Jainism tradition, which is related in a number of books by Osho. I read it in *Fear: Understanding and Accepting the Insecurities of Life*. The tale is of a chakravartin – an all-powerful leader of the whole earth: the wheels of his chariot can move anywhere. It was said that after his death, a chakravartin would be able to sign his name on a hallowed mountain made of pure gold in heaven; this mount, 'Sumeru', is so beautiful it makes Mount Everest look pathetic. Hearing this, the chakravartin looked forward to death, but wondered where the fun was in signing his name if no one could watch him? He ordered his entire kingdom to kill themselves upon his death, so he could have an audience.

When he dies, he goes up to the gates of heaven with all his kingdom in tow – queens, courtiers, citizens – and is greeted by a gatekeeper, who orders him to leave everyone at the gate. The chakravartin is confused and irritated, but the gatekeeper promises him that he would prefer this upon seeing the mountain. The gatekeeper tells him that every chakravartin has brought a huge number of people with him and every chakravartin who heeded his advice has been grateful for it. So the chakravartin follows the gatekeeper, leaving his posse at the gate. Upon reaching the golden mountain, it is indeed better than anything he imagined. The gatekeeper hands him a special pen to sign his name, but as the chakravartin approaches, he sees the golden mountain is covered with names. There is no space to write.

He is humbled by this – he'd believed himself to be special in reaching this point, only to find that millions of people have been here before him. Then the caretaker of the mountain tells him that the only way to sign his name is to erase another name. Osho writes that, upon hearing this, 'the whole joy was gone, the whole excitement was gone . . .' The chakravartin said to the man 'It just means someone else will come tomorrow and he will erase my name.' The mountain caretaker confirms this is indeed the case; they have to do so, or there isn't enough space. The chakravartin refuses to sign – seeing the pointlessness of it all – and promises to go back to the gate, where, instead of bragging, he shares the wisdom of what he has seen.[28]

I'm telling this story because social media is a powerful challenge for our ego. Many use it to look good and therefore feel good, thrilled to have an audience that they can brag to, similar to the chakravartin wanting to sign his name on the golden mountain. This is further amplified by the dopamine-flavoured reward of social validation: notifications.

This is how social media becomes addictive: we get a little hit – not quite enough to satisfy – and we keep going back for more. Have you ever found yourself on the feedback merry-go-round, checking Instagram, then Facebook, then Twitter, around and around jabbing the refresh button again, and again, and again? Hours of the day can be lost on the online carousel. At its worst, the carousel becomes toxic – especially when we don't get the attention we crave – or we compare ourselves to others, whom we believe are getting the attention and happiness we don't or can't have. We feel less worthy, our lives lacking.

Social-media activity is not a symbol of your worth. It's not a substitute for a social life, or face-to-face contact (as anyone in a long-distance relationship will tell you). Neither does it offer a true representation of someone's life or even their true character. Technology has evolved more rapidly than our social skills can keep pace with. The power of social media also threatens our ability to develop genuine self-awareness and (especially challenging for teenagers) the chance to develop a balanced, realistic self-image and acceptance. Once we are alert to and self-protective against this, we can use these tools to the reverse: enhancing our communication skills, learning how to build healthy relationships.

Now, more people than ever have public platforms to share their work, their creativity, opinions, thoughts and feelings. We now see and hear the millions of voices (and smartphones) raised against societal, economic, political or sexual oppression. With this, we see a huge cultural shift towards redefining and policing unacceptable behaviour, both on and offline. That's where social media offers us real value; affording us a level of insight into the way we act, individually, as members of a community, and as humans in the world, who can spark important real-life conversations, leading to sweeping social change and progress.

Building relationships in the community

The most obvious point that everyone misses is that you get back what you put out there, in terms of emotional content. The way people respond to you is a reflection of what you're communicating. We know this instinctively – when we meet someone happy, we start to feel uplifted and share happy memories and thoughts with them. When someone starts telling us a story full of anger, we start to feel angry, too. Human beings mirror each other. It takes a large degree of self-awareness to remain in your own emotional state rather than latch on to someone else's (see Boundaries, page 103).

What this means is, if you post 'angry' content online, it is likely you will receive anger back. Sometimes this will be from a follower sharing your anger, but sometimes it will be from someone angry with you. That's perfectly okay, but if you don't want to handle anger, try adjusting your language and lowering the emotional temperature of your posts. Similarly, more positive posts generate positive responses. You won't always know whether someone is pleased with what you shared, but it might be someone happy about something else entirely who taps into your shared emotion at that moment; or maybe a friend who is just happy you're there.

All this being said, you can share whatever you want – just share *consciously*. Notice how your posts affect how you are received online and experiment. If you don't agree with a post, and you usually just nod along and ignore it, tell someone you don't agree. See how that feels. See how they respond.

Paradoxically, though it certainly enables us to edit ourselves, social media is also a way to be more *you* – to find your voice and to share yourself with others. See what happens when you say something a little different. Be vulnerable. Make friends with people, tell them when you enjoy their posts, let them know if something was valuable to you and how it affected you. Maybe even send them a private message. If you find you are regularly communicating well with someone, arrange to meet in real life. Join online groups that match your interests and add your opinion to the conversation. Remember also that it can be educational to connect with people who have different viewpoints to you. Perhaps you'll learn something!

I'm lucky enough not to get many nasty comments, but when I do (and if I'm in the right headspace), I always try to respond with kindness and curiosity. Ask questions. What do they really mean by their words? Most people are never really angry at you; often there is something else going on in their life causing this upset and you've got caught in the crossfire. The opportunity to be heard can swiftly neutralize their anger.

There are caveats to this: the first is that it's fine to be curious, but if someone's repeated negativity or posts bring you down, and/or they become abusive, you don't have to stay connected with them or respond to their communications. I will say that if you generate enough loving feeling in your community, people will support you, even if there are others who choose to send abuse.

Try your best to avoid firing off angry posts in the heat of the moment. Knee-jerk reactions are inevitable at times – everyone has triggers. However, a good maxim I used when I was teaching social-media management is: 'Don't post when you're pissed or pissed off.' We lose awareness at these times, and can end up inscribing a fleeting emotion on the stone tablet of the internet, a place where (terrifyingly) everything is permanently accessible.

At a distance, we can divorce ourselves from reality and forget that there *are* others (with very real feelings) who we can easily harm in the supposed 'echo chambers' into which we shout. Similarly, we can be hurt and shamed, when this happens to us. We want to engage but we struggle to do it in a way that doesn't sound like an attack, it's a good idea to privately message people. It takes the heat out of the communication, and shows that we are trying to engage and understand them, not publicly humiliate them. This can allow us to learn, and potentially teach someone about our perspective. Ideally, we find validity in both, but if we do not, at least we maximize the opportunity to grow in understanding.

When social media becomes harmful

When does social media stop becoming a useful exercise in communication and observation – an enjoyable way to catch up with friends – and instead start taking away from and not adding to your life? When not going on it makes you feel uncomfortable. It is now a habit and a distraction, sapping energy from you, maybe even making you feel isolated and lonely (more on this later).

Some of us, without realizing it, end up in a semi-abusive relationship with our phones. We rely on social-media notifications for validation, and to give us a feeling of accomplishment or activity. We check for them first thing in the morning and last thing at night; we stay longer on apps than we wanted to, and lose hours scrolling mindlessly to feed a feeling we didn't even realize we had. We can't sleep, our head's buzzing. If you find yourself in a social-media loop (check Twitter: nothing happening; move on to Facebook: not much; on to Instagram: check again – and back round again), then it's likely something is going on that isn't so healthy.

I remember having a little bit of an addiction to social media while working as a journalist. I would spend hours trawling Twitter in the evening, pretending to myself that it was for work, when really it was just because I didn't quite know what to do with myself. I began to notice that I picked up my phone to check social media whenever I had an uncomfortable feeling. I didn't want to leave my phone outside of the bedroom at night. Social media became another way I was avoiding being with myself, and on top of that it was fragmenting my attention even further, making it even harder to plan what I wanted to do with my free time.

If any of this sounds like you, there are some really easy, simple, changes you can make to wean yourself off social media:

- *Do not make it the first thing you check in the morning.*
- *Make a promise to yourself that you will have your first hot drink of the day, take a few breaths and give yourself some space before you start filling up on it again.*
- *Give yourself a social-media curfew. You can make a ritual out of it. At 10 p.m., lovingly switch off your phone and put it in a little box to sleep. Let yourself uncurl out of the day without fighting it with screen-time.*
- *Only check it a maximum of three times a day. The benefit of this is you'll have much more to see when you do check in.*
- *Turn off notifications. If needs be, remove the apps from your phone. You can also put your phone in grayscale, which turns everything black and white, and removes the desire to stay very long on it as it's far less attractive and stimulating.*

Social media is a wonderful way to learn about the world and about how humans communicate, to build communities, and to stay connected. But it's a very poor compensation for a life lived offline, and the relationships and communities we build as physical beings, not digital ones.

WHERE YOU LIVE

There's one community you're part of by default; and that is the people who live where you live. It seems a bit nostalgic to talk of local community these days, what with an increase in renting, jobs becoming more mobile, greater migration and people seeking refugee status. Certainly this idea of a strong community made up of the same group of people who share a permanent space they call home is changing. There are 258 million people living in a country that is not their own, according to a 2017 UN report.

On top of that, transport links mean we often work far away from where we live, our friends live on the other side of town and our homes become nothing more than accommodation: places where we eat and sleep (until we retire). How much time do you have to spend somewhere before a location becomes local? And how much longer than that before you describe yourself as 'a local'?

It's not really about time. It's about commitment. The two are interlinked, though. When everyone seems to be simply passing through, and even you yourself don't know how long you'll be living in a certain locale, investing time and energy in a place – getting to know the people around you or what's happening in your neighbourhood seems a little precocious. I get it – taking good care of your immediate surroundings when no one else seems to bother, or contributing to maintenance or upkeep when you're barely ever there, seems like a fool's errand. Making new friends and investigating what's going on in a new place feels scary – 'I hate small talk – what if the neighbours are weird? Then I'll have to say hi to weirdos for the rest of my life.'

The result of having an inner monologue like this? Loneliness. Either for you or for the people around you.

And loneliness is a killer. I could quote stats at you (extreme loneliness increases a person's chances of premature death by 14 per cent according to one study[29]), but frankly, we all know how awful feeling lonely is. Isolation in crowds can creep up on us slowly. We don't register how disconnected we are in our homes until we get locked out and realize we don't know anyone we'd feel comfortable having a cup of tea with until the locksmith arrives.

The purpose of this section is to explain why it's worth giving a f**k about where you live, taking part in local activities, and getting to know the people close by. Even if you don't feel like it, even if you don't think you'll be living there long, and even if you think your street does not contain 'your sort of people' – even if you think no one is interested. Let's stop our world from being full of passing ghosts attached to their phones instead of the space and people around them.

You're affecting and affected by your local community, even if you don't realize it

At the end of the nineteenth century, a handsome Frenchman was conducting research into forensics in Lyon, in the first CSI laboratory in the world, which he had fought hard with the local police department to set up. His name was Dr Edmond Locard and he became known as the Sherlock Holmes of France.

He formulated one of the basic principles of forensic science known as Locard's exchange principles, also known as 'every contact leaves a trace'. He asserted something that is now held as gospel in forensics: that whatever or wherever someone has been, if there has been contact, they will have left something behind. If a burglar has been in your house, they will have left something behind. If a murder has been committed, there has been some exchange of forensic material. In every contact between people and place, from person to person, something is left behind. It might be invisible to the naked eye but it doesn't mean it's not there.

Let's think about what this means for the places we live. If even on crime scenes, where a perpetrator spends only a short period of time and wants to wipe his imprint away, an exchange can be found, then the impact we leave on where we live, even if it is somewhere we wouldn't call home, could be phenomenal in comparison.

If everywhere we rest for a while is affected by us in some way or another, then we have options: do you want to be the sort of person who when they come into contact with a place, makes it better? Or do you want to make it worse? Whatever happens, you're leaving a trace – it doesn't matter how long you stay there for. So take control of that trace. Be part of something in a good way. Actually 'live' in your local community.

There's knowing this cognitively, and then there's feeling it. Especially when a place still feels foreign and strange to you. I call it having alien eyes. Alien eyes make you feel under attack. It's that disorientating feeling when you get out of the airport and worry that people are going to mug you, the taxi driver is overcharging you, or the rented apartment feels cold and actively hostile, like it actually wants you to feel lonely. The revolting picture on the wall of the kitchen feels like a personal attack.

Luckily, alien eyes are easily cured. The smallest act can change all this and have you feel part of a place; choosing to pick up a piece of litter and put it in the bin, smiling at someone on the street, saying hi to the person having coffee next to you, offering to carry someone's shopping bags if they are struggling. I now make it my business to generate as much 'place karma' as possible; leave the places you stay for a while as brilliant or more brilliant than you found them.

Let community work you

It works both ways. This contact between us and a community is an exchange – we affect the community and the community affects us. I believe we absorb a little bit of the places we go and the people we see. If we are influenced by our surroundings no matter what, it makes sense that we become more consciously part of that process so that we can make sure the exchange is a positive one, and that we gain all the benefits of community as part of that trade between ourselves and ourphysical environment.

Some people find the idea of local community incredibly suffocating – they prefer the anonymity and perceived freedom that accompanies independence. I'd argue the opposite: how much more free do you feel if you know you have an entire tribe of support on your doorstep? I'm not denying it can be a challenge to maintain your selfhood, assert your boundaries and not be swayed by worries about the judgement of others in community – but being able to navigate this is an essential part of becoming an adult. Peer pressure and compliance are real, but the price for avoiding these is isolation. Meanwhile, judgement always says more about the person doing the judging than the judged.

It can feel incredibly freeing, too, to discover different parts of yourself: how it's possible to relate to different people, how to learn new skills, and have a pool of people to call on to ask for advice.

Be a member of a number of different communities, so that you can know that the flavour of one group isn't necessarily the same as another and that's okay. Use them to bring out different sides of you. Know that different communities with their different priorities can help you discover how you feel about certain ways of living. It's good to be able to hang out in different places, with different people, depending on how you feel that day. Pick and choose the bits that suit you and leave the rest.

Finding and building communities

Sometimes we move somewhere where there is already a thriving and active community spirit; it's just a case of finding it. If it's not obvious through an internet search, try typing up some relevant search terms into Facebook to look for groups.

If you've still come up empty-handed, then check bulletin boards, or ask people who work locally if they know where you can find out what's going on in the area. Go to the local park and speak with dog owners – usually they know a lot about the area simply because they are out walking the streets and the grassy areas with their pet a lot. Churches or synagogues, temples or mosques, also usually have open events for members of the local community. Keep an open mind. Practise being welcoming and approachable. Assume people want to connect until they tell you they don't. Most people are dying for someone to be interested in what they have to say.

Sometimes we might not be able to find a group that suits our needs. That's okay. Belonging is not always a feeling we're born with, it's something we occasionally have to work at. That's when you can set up your own little community.

Life coach, Caoilfhionn Nic Conmara, brought together a tribe of women for sisterhood brunches after moving from Dublin to London. Every month this group meet at each other's houses, invite new friends they want to introduce to the group, share food and then go and do something local to the area. It's a way of meeting new people, expanding friendship circles and bonding with women in a friendly, sober, non-competitive environment.

'When I was feeling lonely last year, I made it my goal to meet as many new people as possible and make a tribe of friends around me,' she tells me. 'Often when I was feeling especially vulnerable and lonely, I'd ring people up and share how I was feeling, and the resounding answer was always, "OMG, me too, London is a lonely town, we all struggle to feel like we fit in". 'She goes on. 'Realizing that everybody gets lonely in this city, helped spur me on to organize brunches and events with all my disparate friends, in the hope to build a tribe.'

Caoilfhionn Nic Conmara chose women because, 'Many of my female friends were upset at the dearth of deep female friendships and sisterhood. I wanted all of my female friends to become friends and support each other.'

If you want to build your own mini tribe, or start a gathering in your area, I've noticed that these seven ingredients are helpful in sustaining a community. From my own experience, a well-bonded group that supports its members will always observe these precepts:

- *A clear and compelling reason for coming together. The intention of the group is an important statement and something everyone in the group should know and identify with. It should include a 'what' and a 'why'. This is the shared bond – whether it's litter picking and making the local area tidier, or a book group discussing a certain genre of literature to learn more, or even a weight-loss group, where people come together to support each other as they get fitter. There may be other benefits, too (for example, making new friends), but the main intention should be simple and persuasive. This indicates to possible new members why they might want to join and also reminds people already in the community why they are there – for those days when you don't feel like turning up to choir practice or helping pick up litter.*

- *Make it inclusive.* *Choosing to set up a group defined solely by who is not allowed in is the equivalent of making friends to help you build a shrine to your own insecurities. The covert way of doing this is making the barrier to entering the community so difficult that it dissuades people from joining. Chill out. Encourage people to invite their friends. Be welcoming. Encourage members to befriend each other. Set up a buddy system for new people so they have a point of contact. Foster an environment where everyone is greeted as if they were a film star or a long-lost friend. There are not enough hugs and smiles in this world; there's no need to be standoffish and corporate in community.*

- *Arrange regular physical meet-ups.* *Virtual communities are great but they pale in comparison to in-the-flesh meetings. Set a date and time (say the first Saturday of every month) and stick to it. Make it convenient for the group you're in; if childcare is an issue, you might want to choose a different day, for example. Regular dates and times allows people to plan to be there. Check in with people before to ask if they will be able to make it, to jog their memories. Have an online presence, to allow people to communicate in between and build connection. WhatsApp threads or Facebook groups are great for this.*

- *Set up a structure that reinforces inclusivity.* *Icebreakers work. Make sure you get everyone's voice in the room early on or have a system that allows everyone to be heard who wants to be. If the group is small enough, do a round of names or introductions. For larger groups you might want to give out name badges (it's hard to remember and it's embarrassing to keep asking). If it's possible, provide context on who knows who or how long they've been a member – it's easy to feel like the odd one out. Information can work as a peg for people to pick up personal conversations later.*

- **Have guidelines, community rules and etiquette.** *Community guidelines help people feel safe so that they feel they can reveal themselves (for example, a confidentiality or no-judgement rule) and also reaffirm the purpose of the group. Usually the etiquette is there for a reason. For example, in hot yoga, you are asked not to leave the room so that you don't disturb others and stay in the zone. In my orgasmic meditation women's group, where we talk about being sexual as women, they ask us not to indulge in one-downmanship – if one person has had a bad week, it doesn't mean we all need to play down our achievements or happy experiences in order to try and make them feel better. It's something that women often do, so they pre-warn us in order to counter that tendency we have towards sympathetic modesty. These guidelines aren't 'enforceable' as such; they are often just rails to direct the community towards more effective action.*

- **Encourage greater and greater involvement.** *It's a good idea if you can in some way share different roles around the group so that one week one person is leading, and another week someone else is. It not only feels 'fair' and gives people different experiences, but also lets everyone become more invested in the community. It also stops a false hierarchy* *from developing among older members of the group, or the running of the community becoming onerous if left to one or two people. If the group expands in numbers, establishing a committee might be the way forward – you could even make the committee a rolling one. Donations or other contributions can also help people invest more – putting money into something is one way people come to feel part of it.*

● *Make it fun. No one wants to take part in something that becomes a chore; too restrictive, or overly dogmatic. Bring joy into the group, even if it's serious. Encourage socializing before and after events and ties between members. With many communities I've been a part of, I've signed up for one thing, and ended up coming back again and again for the friends I've made and the fun it is to hang out together.*

The brilliant thing about building a community where you live is that you always have a baseline interest in common to build on: your shared location. That sounds great, but actually there's nothing like close contact to produce friction. Take it as a given; you're annoying at times and your neighbours are going to be annoying at times. The more things you have in common, the more annoying they'll be (there's nothing like sharing a front door to dramatically increase how objectively awful someone is; it's truly fascinating). There will be times where you are comforted only by the realization that you are also as annoying to them as they are to you.

There's always a way through, and it's in both your interests to find it. When you do, the rewards for navigating that tough situation will be greater, too. In my experience, the more possessive you are, the more problems you're going to have. Step back. Caring here does not mean controlling or getting fixated; it means wanting to make things better.

The best thing about caring in community is that it is contagious. There's a woman on my street who, simply because she likes gardening, has dug up around the trees in our little cul-de-sac and planted all kinds of flowers. Now we have daffodils on our road instead of old fried-chicken bones and weeds and cigarette butts. Every time I see these flowers it's a reminder to me that anything we do that improves an environment for us, also has an impact on others that extends beyond the action itself. They work as an inspiration, or an invitation for us all to do a little to make where we live that much brighter. I'm grateful to her not just for making our two streets look prettier, but for reminding me to care.

Infinity
and Beyond

GIVE A F**K
ABOUT INFINITY
AND BEYOND

Caring about the wider world used to feel totally overwhelming for me. Chaotic, unmanageable and exhausting. Most of the time it was out of my range to care about anything other than whatever current turbulence was running my life and absorbing my attention. There were some occasional moments in the small hours between sleeping and waking when bigger questions about the world and who I was, in a macro, more magical sense, would germinate in my dreamy mind, but I would forget them promptly upon waking and get to work instead being busy with the drama-du-jour.

My lack of interest in the world bothered me a bit, but I put it down to simply being a bit of a self-absorbed person, one of the many flawed, egocentric humans I saw in the world who couldn't give much of a toss outside their own sphere. Even their posts on Facebook professing altruism were nothing more than a performance of goodness. I was a very cynical human, and I saw vanity, ignorance, anger and pride all around me. I didn't want to give a f★★k because I thought it was hopeless and I thought it wasn't worth it.

I have come to realize I was wrong to judge myself in this way and I was wrong about the nature of humanity. I fundamentally do care about this planet and had the desire to care even back then – it's just I had some housekeeping to do on myself before that was possible. I think a lot of us feel this way, to a certain extent, and we could be a bit more compassionate with each other while we go through that process.

The reason I was so tense and anxious about the world was that the way I felt about myself was off, my relationships with other people were disconnected and I had no community. Essentially, how I felt about myself mirrored my general confusion and resentment towards the universe and all that was in it. If I had told myself back then that I could care so actively about the world and it could feel glorious, I would have thought it impossible. That's why this section is last, after the advice about how to give a f★★k about relating to yourself and others, because, in St Francis of Assisi's words: 'Start by doing what's necessary; then do what's possible; and suddenly you are doing the impossible.'

It's not about perfection – totally nailing the self-love, being a distinguished boundary-setter and becoming hailed as a community leader before you start to relate consciously to the wider world (although having a strong platform of self-care, friends and feeling part of something will help anchor you on this journey). What we believe about the world and our place within it will inform how we behave in all those other areas, and these in turn will affect how we relate to the wider world.

When I talk about the wider world, I'm looking at the bigger-picture things that influence our everyday lives but that we rarely stop and consider thoughtfully. Some are more tangible – like the news and money. Others are more abstract and philosophical – like what our purpose is, or where we find meaning. What we think about love, pain and humanity – our worldview. All of these things are incredibly important to give a f★★k about, and to investigate why they are important to us. Then we can adjust our relationship to them to serve us and the world better.

First, the news – we watch it, read it, listen to it, and discuss topics that come up, but short of straightforward complaining, we don't actually think about why we care about the news or what it gives us. And because we don't do that, we can't examine how to give a f★★k about it in such a way that we aren't stuck between despair and anger at the media and instead can be provided with a news service that does what it is meant to: illuminate global and local issues that are important, in an interesting and informative way.

Similarly, we exchange money every day, but how many of us stop and think about our relationship to money itself and how it might be holding us back? Holding us back from making more; holding us back from valuing ourselves and our services; holding us back from making friends – maybe ones who aren't in the same financial bracket; holding us back from pitching for great things in front of great people? Most of us do care about money, but in a way that only serves to dishonour ourselves and others. Like news, we have a habit of making it too important, or disconnecting from it altogether. Money is a taboo topic; let's drag it out from under the jealous dragon and examine our attitudes to it so that we can be free and generous in our financial dealings, rather than tight, defensive and constrained.

Because money and news are visible, loud presences in our lives, it may seem like they have more impact on who we are and what we do than the more ephemeral matters of finding a sense of purpose and nurturing a positive worldview. However, on a more subterranean level, these big questions inform everything we think, feel and do. They direct our lives, almost invisibly, from the very depths of us. It may seem daunting to ask ourselves how we feel about such deep subjects, especially when no answers seem immediately forthcoming. It's true – some people have made investigating these questions their life's work. However, just being willing to sit with these topics is a process that lets us peel back layers of conditioning and fear, many of which have long outgrown their use, so that we can get in touch with the beauty that's deep within us.

There's this curious thing about examining how we feel about the wider world – it puts us more in touch with the core of who we really are, which then helps us reconnect with the wider world in a way that's more authentic, present, invested and enjoyable. That's when caring starts to feel good, almost automatic; an effortless part of being, fundamental to who you are. Plugging into this bigger picture we feel connected to ourselves, to people around us, to the community we live in and to the world. Giving a f★★k about the wider world is really just a beautiful way to care for yourself.

THE NEWS

Before I tell you why you need to care about the news, let me declare my bias. I am a former full-time member of the mainstream media (MSM). I care deeply about news and about the way people engage with it. I've spent most of the last decade trying (quite successfully, ultimately) to get people to read, listen to and watch the news that myself and my colleagues produce. Persuading people to engage with and value the news they consume is vital to ensuring its proper production, and properly produced news can change the world.

Saying that, I also know there is such a thing as caring too much – or caring 'unhealthily' about the news. I stopped working in rolling news not only because it exposed me to a boiling cauldron of pain, fear and constant disaster, but also because I could feel it cause ripples of trauma across social media; an avalanche of negative news affecting the nation's emotional state. I know an awful lot about the effects of over-consumption of news – if you're looking for an expert on how to relate to current affairs in a way that will damage your mental health, I'm your woman. That's why caring about the news is not enough – it's *how* you care about it that counts.

I also left current affairs because I dislike the way the current media model operates, perhaps just as much as those who moan about the news online every day.

Fundamentally, though, I can see how much brilliant news reporting there is – despite the difficult conditions – and I'm continually grateful for being able to access information about the world around me in real time, from sources I (more or less) trust. I'm not denying there are problems. The media isn't perfect, but the solution is not to switch off and care less, it's to care more.

We need to care about the news for five crucial reasons: to find out what's going on that affects us (if we want to live in this world it's helpful to know what's going on in it); to make a change and have impact; to stretch our perspective and introduce us to new ideas; to connect with others and feel part of the whole; and also to learn from mistakes.

'Hear ye, hear ye'

Bulletins, newspapers and push updates have a very basic practical function, a bit like the town crier of old. The media provides a shared space where issues that affect us can be raised and discussed. Where else can you make announcements or let people know what's going on? Sure, we can send people letters, or do group texts, but what if you don't have that information? How do you get a message out?

> Lots of newspapers have 'gazette' in the title because the first Venetian newspapers, in the sixteenth century, cost one '*gazzetta*' – a Venetian coin.

It's no good howling at the moon when something happens if you've disengaged with all the discussions leading up to it. In fact, when changes are not adequately publicized, people suffer adversely. In some countries, governments restrict press freedom, controlling the flow of information to repress their people. This is one role that the news plays in our lives – it serves as a kind of information forum, where we can check in and see what is happening that may affect us or people we love. No one wants to eat a horse-meat lasagne if they don't need to.

Additionally, the pressure of publicity can force change – when things are dragged into the light, people can come together against it. Before Edward Snowden leaked documents about the NSA collecting data, causing a worldwide scandal, it wasn't known that the USA had been mass monitoring global communications. It was even reported that Angela Merkel's cell phone had been monitored – leading to the German Chancellor calling Barack Obama, president at the time, and telling him (according to reports) that 'spying on friends is never acceptable'. Another recent example of publicity forcing change in the UK is that of the Windrush scandal – the treatment of people who arrived from the

Caribbean between 1948 and 1970, who were threatened with deportation (in some cases actually deported) in error due to new bureaucratic rules designed to deter other immigrants in 2012. Their appalling treatment had been happening for years without a national uproar. Caribbean leaders had complained to the UK government about these enforced deportations of older people who had lived legally in the country, paying tax and National Insurance for over fifty years, only to be put on a plane to Jamaica when in their seventies. It wasn't until fresh cases were reported in the press, embarrassing the Home Office and fuelling public anger, that changes began to be made to benefit these citizens.

The news explodes our perspective – not only might we hear of events in our local area that otherwise we wouldn't hear about, of things that might interest or affect us, but also we hear of issues in places we may never visit.

The world continually challenges our imagination with its possibilities, and when it's not priests, drug dealers or shamans bending our reality then it's journalists who often wear the winged sandals, reporting facts stranger than fiction. The metaphor 'a black swan' was used in Europe (as far back as the Roman poet Juvenal) to mean something that didn't exist. Which was all lovely and clever and satirical until Europeans began to settle in Australia and discovered that black swans did in fact exist. How embarrassing. If only there had been CNN!

I'm being facetious. The colour of swans may not impact on our lives so much, but this term has been re-popularized by Nassim Nicholas Taleb in his book, *The Black Swan: The Impact of the Highly Improbable*[30], to describe things that we can't predict because they are unlike our previous experiences. There are still a lot of questions about the world that we are yet to answer, both individually and collectively. We don't even know what to google because we have no reference point for it. And yet, if we don't acknowledge them, or seek to uncover them, they can derail us. Reading the news is one way we can begin to familiarize ourselves with the unexpected, and broaden our own experience of the world so that we have more data to base our decisions on, adjusting our relationship to the world and widening our perspectives.

We find out about space travel, electric cars, and kings under car parks. We are told of volcanoes erupting, of plane crashes, of cougar attacks, of refugee camps, of Ebola and Zika. We hear about what's captivating conversation in countries besides our own – other cities; of crimes that have sent shockwaves through international cultures; and we face the headlines that affect our local communities, too. The news tells us of things that immediately concern and affect us, and things that appear not to. It illuminates the differences between cultures and also allows us to see our shared humanity, if we allow it. Grief looks the same on faces the world over, even if mourning takes a different ritual form. News allows us to connect with others, both near and far, and helps us feel connected to the whole. This happens on a very visceral level in coffee shops – if people are discussing the weather, then they're talking about something in the news. It's something we share and use to connect.

Media-reporting influences our lives, no matter how far away it is; the headlines affect the beliefs and behaviours of those around us, the economy and the emotional temperature of society. It is almost impossible to remain in our own bubble any more – it would mean avoiding the internet, social media and news-stands, and only coming into contact with people who do the same. We live and operate in a space shared with others, who are also affected by the news – the markets and our moods are subtly shifting all the time. What's reported becomes part of our collective landscape whether we like it or not.

In short, Toto, not only are we are not in Kansas any more, but whatever happens in Munchkinland is going to affect Aunt Em and Uncle Henry back home, as well as impact on the trees in the Haunted Forest and quite possibly blow up Emerald City, too. Globalization is here and it doesn't give a f★★k if you want to elect Trump or vote for Brexit. We are connected now, and it will take the heart, courage and brains of all of us to see this one through.

The best possible scenario is that we all learn from each other, developing respect, love and cooperation. The worst possible scenario is that we don't – and if one country goes down, we all go down in the ensuing tornado. The news is a bit like monogamy or democracy: it's not ideal and it fails us repeatedly, but for most of us, it's marginally better than the alternative, which is not knowing a damn thing and completely disengaging with the world and what it's currently reading, watching and talking about.

Knowing what's going on out there allows us to see and feel opportunities to care more. Places where our skills might be needed for what interests us – there might even be a place where you see how you can set up a business or offer a service. News organizations are great for alerting us to top-level information – it is up to us what we do next at ground level. Discover an event where people are talking about an issue. Sign up. Buy a book. Embrace the crazy and see if there's hidden genius there. Learn from the history, the mistakes, what came before the reported event and why people think the way they do. News is not necessarily only top level – it's just what is new. There's always going to be more to it than can be contained in the latest update.

What's wrong with the news

My experience of people who criticize the media in its entirety is that they have a fundamental misunderstanding of how the news is forced to operate and its reliance on the audience to direct its output. You might as well criticize capitalism or humanity, or, dare I say it, the nature of reality.

The way the news is delivered is in flux right now. No one knows more than the media the difficulty with the current model. The idea that you could report 'the facts' as they happen, globally, twenty-four hours a day, seven days a week, on demand, for free, with excellent visual data and succinct analysis, is a problematic one at best. Philosophers and historians still clash over what the truth is, but yes, sure, a thirty-five-year-old reporter, with a camera, in a war zone, is definitely going to be able to get to the bottom of it by 6 p.m. so it can make the bulletin.

Of course, there's a limit to what's knowable, but there are some facts that are beyond dispute too. That doesn't mean we should stop engaging with the news – it just means we need to adjust our relationship to it. To see it as the gateway to greater knowledge, rather than reading headlines as signs saying 'the truth stops here', with flashing arrows to the copy underneath.

There is a lot wrong with the news and journalists, but Lord, don't audiences like to moan about things journalists can't control. Sometimes the feedback is helpful: when someone points out an inaccuracy or that some phrasing in a headline or article was poor. But you really can't please everyone. In my experience, sometimes people would be so angry that the BBC wasn't reporting something properly (we were, they just couldn't find it up high enough on the website) or wasn't reporting it at all (we were trying to – there was no conspiracy: we would be aware of it; it was merely that we were trying to check it was true, or that the source was actually legitimate and worth trusting). Or maybe their 'story' just wasn't sufficiently important to the nation – people simply didn't care enough.

That's the thing audiences don't understand. We report what *you* want to hear about, what you share and what you read; even more these days, because we have the data on what is popular. Even more so because of the way algorithms work, because peer-reviewed news is now the way we consume, so the most-read stories become even more most read.

Stop reading the news because you're bored – or you'll only read the most entertaining, shocking, titillating, curious pieces with the silly headlines that misrepresent the serious article. Don't share it to show how silly it is.

Do not read what you do not want produced. Do not share articles you think are fundamentally awful. Even screenshots. Don't joke about them.

Stop making awful people famous because you love to position yourself in opposition to them, either to laugh at them or to show people that you're trustworthy and A Good Person. It is an attention economy online – the free news market only wants eyeballs. Stop giving attention to things you don't like and don't want. (That's a good philosophy for life, not just for news.)

Editors try not to cater to the lowest common denominator, but audiences don't often help. We'll spend time and money trying to make you read something about Yemen, but if you don't read it or share it, we'll stop investing, until someone pipes up in news conference again and makes a case for why we should do it anyway. If you want news coverage, get a campaign group together and make a pact to share everything on it. Get Facebook groups, Twitter lists, numbers. Get good pictures. Then journalists will start covering all your issues. That is how it works. It's not about people getting the media they deserve, it's that people get the media they click on, share

– and are willing to pay for.

Buy your news. It might feel a bit chicken and egg: 'I hate the media, why should I pay for it?' But just hang on with the economics for a second. Free online readers are worth so little to publishers that the sheer numbers needed on every article to allow the organization to survive are immense. It means a large volume of articles have to be produced, which means a quick turnaround, which means no time to research or take care. That means attention grabbing and quick hits and the news you love to hate.

What bias?

When I worked online, I usually saw about seven main gripes from readers, broadly grouped into 'That's not true'; 'That headline is misleading'; 'That's not newsworthy'; 'Why aren't you reporting on [insert other story]'; 'Fake news' and 'You're biased'. Obviously, pointing out whether something is true or not can be helpful. Sometimes a different view on a headline, if it's alienating readers, can be useful feedback too. The newsworthy one is a uselessly subjective complaint that really irritates me because we know as journalists that it's not serious news; we also know from watching our analytics that you're damn well reading it in droves; far above our in-depth reporting on trade tariffs and prison reform.

However, the gripe about bias is one I always think is the most ridiculous, although it's obviously valid and skewers all media organizations. It even messes with ones like the BBC that try and offset it with opposing voices and end up overcompensating: allowing people who are simply racist or wrong a large amount of airtime in order to provide 'balance'. The most I think we can ever do is declare and know our biases as much as possible.

We are all biased: sometimes we can become conscious of our prejudices and sometimes, we have bias blind spots that no matter how hard we try, we fail to see. Every reader has bias. Every journalist has bias. Sometimes people shout fake news when they really mean 'we do not share the same bias!'

I'm a woman – I'm going to feel more engaged with certain equality issues. I'm white – I'm almost definitely going to have less cultural or emotional investment – and even, dare I say it, more implicit bias – while reporting on stories that focus on race, compared with someone from another ethnic background (it's why diverse newsrooms are so important). Those are some biases I can work to eradicate or compensate for when I cover certain stories, so that I interview different people with different viewpoints from mine; then have an editor and another editor check and double-check to see if I'm leaking any implicit bias.

Many companies are now training staff about diversity by having an implicit bias test that can assess whether, despite your best intentions, you have some automatic preferences; that check, for example, if you are biased against LGBT, the obese, the disabled or people from another race. This is particularly important for those recruiting for the business, as automatic bias can see the most talented people not hired for a role, simply because of their background and the bias of those in HR.

Journalists do the best they can not to let bias affect their work, so they put out only what is closest to objective as possible, but there are always limits. For example, say you are reporting from Iraq but being escorted by the US army – which you may have to be for safety reasons: you can only get detail from a certain viewpoint.

Be curious and caring about this by reading at least three different sources of news – don't just take one article as fact. Be aware that lots of papers use the same wire service – this means that media organizations pay for an independent company to send its journalists out and report back bald facts. We are all using the same sources sometimes.

If something interests you it's great to seek out opinion pieces that can help adjust the lens through which you are viewing events. Be aware, though: a compelling writer with a persuasive arguing style does not necessarily a truth-teller make.

Changing our relationship

The news poses an almost insurmountable challenge to us. This goes beyond the challenge of absorbing the sheer volume of information available. It's harder than the dilemma of sifting through what is true, what might be true and what is almost definitely not. It's even more difficult than acknowledging our own individual bias and adjusting the lens through which we observe events unfolding in the world today. The news rocks our sense of certainty and power. It makes us feel insignificant, and it hits us right in that terrible spot where instability and panic overwhelm us: 'I don't know, I didn't know, I don't understand, and I have no idea what to do next' are words that no one ever wants to hear, think or say in the face of catastrophe.

Journalists, analysts and audiences all fall victim to our fear of the uncertain, and the unknowable. And to soothe us, politics and personality step in to fill the gap, sweeping in with a simplistic sound bite for a complex problem. Mark Twain said: 'Politicians and diapers must be changed often, and for the same reason.' It's probably not entirely fair to say they are full of sh★t, but they are certainly full of fear. Why else would you – how even could you – blame or shame others for getting it wrong or profess to have a solution in the way that most politicians do? Or even front-page headline writers? We are so afraid of the unknown, we'd rather know familiar suffering, pain, blame and shame. We create one-dimensional villains and flash-in-the-pan heroes. At least we can understand them. At least they are familiar.

Care about the issues. We *need* to care about science, technology, the environment, health, housing, discrimination, conflict and business – but don't get side-tracked by politics. They may seem inseparable but they are not. If we stripped away the politics of *how*, most of us could agree on a *what* – a better quality of life, less crime, more peace, less poverty, more wealth, less ignorance, more knowledge, less hate, more love.

Politics peddles how each party or political ethos has one

plan for what to do next. Unfortunately, that one plan also comes with an identity and a wholesale philosophy. Sign up to one thing and you have to sign up to the whole lot. How crazy is that? We'd never have relationships with anyone if we had to go about our personal lives that way. 'Oh I can only like you if I like everything about you. Sorry, I'm not going to agree with you on this, because if I agree with you on this, I have to agree with you on everything.' It's madness. Terrible people have good ideas. Good people have terrible ideas. It doesn't have to turn into a competition about who is responsible and who is the worst – rather, let's look at the problem and be open to solutions; even if the solutions are complicated and demand nuance. Apologies if it's not as good a story.

All of this is to say, we can be better than backseat drivers when it comes to the news. Instead of loudly grumbling to the other passengers about how crap the driver is, see if he's taking you where you want to go. If not, start googling better directions and decide where you want to end up. Read longer pieces. Get curious. Learn about the issue, talk to people who know about the issue, get informed. Seek areas of agreement rather than gleefully lecturing someone else on how wrong they are. Don't just bitch and carp online about how crap the media is and how everyone is corrupt. You have more power than you think to shape the way your friends, family, colleagues and peers feel or think about issues important to you; but if you channel all that passion and provocation into ranting into the abyss of a comments forum, the power is wasted.

Pledges for good news reading:

- *I will click, read or share the type of news I want to see more of.*
- *I will pay for quality journalism.*
- *I will aim for impartiality, reading more than one news source and looking at more than one viewpoint on issues that are important to me.*
- *I will investigate and be interested in my own bias.*
- *I will share the news I care about.*
- *I will not check or read the news more than three times a day.*
- *I will connect and share with my friends news that interests me and ask for second opinions.*
- *I will remember that there are limits to what the news can provide.*

MONEY

I'm a spiritual person, but I like nice shoes. Free-range eggs cost more, and organic, fair-trade vegetables don't come cheap. I like to buy books and I am a big fan of further education. I enjoy doing yoga, having coaching and time out to do nothing but dance in my pyjamas.

All of this is to say that, in my experience, having money is a good thing. Plus, frankly, cheap wine tastes like crap (although you can still have a lot of fun on it).

There is a certain brand of disciple that might pooh-pooh

my materialism. Let me clarify: I'm not suggesting you get attached to the expensive hairdresser, fluffy towels or the Tempur mattress – enjoying your life doesn't need to be dependent on any conditions, especially not material ones. I agree that true freedom is not needing the latest edition or the nice yoga mat or the high-speed internet (although trying to work on a google doc with low connectivity would make even the Dalai Lama swear, I'd wager). But I enjoy having money and I like the easy opportunities it gives me to experience certain things in life. Plus, who am I kidding? I enjoy the comfort and the pleasure of it all. I'm an extrovert – the advantages of monkish existence have always been a hard sell to me.

There are, of course, ways to spend your money that are more nourishing than others, and a large bank balance doesn't mean happiness. You're going to feel desperate in a different way if you're isolated or don't have nourishing relationships. There are benefits of having less money, too, and I'll get on to those later. However, I'd argue for the general assumption that food, safety and shelter are basic requirements for profitable human existence, and money helps us get those.

Cash is not the be-all and end-all, but it damn well feels that way if you need it. It's hard to be spiritual if you're in a high-rise apartment with five hungry children and the TV turned up loud to drown out the drugs bust next door. 'Use the sound of domestic violence to bring you even deeper into the present,' said no meditation app ever.

My basic philosophy on money is simple: having money is

useful and having more of it, even more so. Swapping money for goods and services is one way we can access things to improve our lives and those of other people. That's why we should give a f★★k about money.

Most of us do care about it, particularly how much we have, how much other people have and whether those two amounts match (although we wouldn't admit it, at least not in polite company). Money is so taboo, people would rather talk about death, politics, religion, sex – anything. In relationships, we sleep with someone before telling them how much we earn. Letting someone touch our genitals is less intimate than letting someone glimpse our bank statement. It's fair to say we have some shame around money.

Perhaps we should, if, as the biblical phrase tells us: 'Money is the root of all evil.' Unfortunately, however, that is a misquotation that's had us crippled with financial embarrassment for hundreds of years. The actual quote in 1 Timothy 6.10 is: 'For the love of money is a root of all kinds of evil.' It's not money that's the root of all evil, it's what we end up thinking about money that scuppers us, whether we're rich or poor, or a member of the smug-as-hell middle classes.

Problem is, if we won't talk about or look at it, we can't really begin to understand how we relate to it and adjust those beliefs to serve us better. Most people think and care about money in such a way that it doesn't help them make it, spend it, donate it or build connections with people who have more or less money than them.

Money, in and of itself, is incredibly useless. In the past you could exchange your bank note for actual gold (which, by the way, is also pretty useless; tried washing your hair with gold? Making pasta with gold? Driving to town on some gold?). However, now you can't even make that exchange. A bank note is simply an IOU from the treasury. It's plastic and metal. Money is only valuable as long as we all agree that it is.

And we do agree on that: money is one of the ways we signify value in our society. It's not the only way, though – so don't get too side-tracked equating price with value; especially because money means different things to different people. The same amount of physical cash can be considered expensive or cheap depending on the relative importance of the goods or service it is exchanged for in one person's perception. Other ways we show value can be with the quality of our attention, sharing our skills with others, our time, our trust, by qualifications, through respect and through love. For some people, taking the time to teach someone something would be a far greater compliment than paying them a lump sum. It's very personal; we all make money mean different things.

The truth is, the amount of money you have in your bank account means ... that is how much money you have in your bank account. It does not mean you have no talent, no power, no resources or no worth. You, as a human being, don't lose or gain anything in terms of intrinsic value depending on how much money you have. We seem to forget that, though, and wrap money in lots of different stories that don't benefit us.

Tick how many of these you agree with:

- *Richer people are less generous with their money.*
- *Poorer people are more loving.*
- *Richer people are stuck-up.*
- *Richer people are more well educated.*
- *Poorer people haven't made the most of their opportunities.*
- *Richer people haven't experienced life.*
- *Rich people don't understand what it is like to be poor.*
- *Poorer people have more of an appreciation for things.*
- *Richer people are just lucky.*
- *Richer people are a slave to their possessions.*
- *Life has been unfair to poor people.*
- *Rich people don't understand the meaning of life.*
- *I judge how people spend their money.*
- *I judge how successful someone is according to how much money they have.*
- *I find it uncomfortable hanging out with people who have much more or much less than me.*
- *I wouldn't let anyone see my bank balance.*
- *I think people in debt are foolish/irresponsible.*

Are you getting a picture of where you stand with money? We heap all this meaning onto rich and poor but there are so many different, contradictory views about money that it ceases to have any meaning at all, other than what it can buy. Our view on money doesn't even reflect our financial situation – it's not even ours most of the time.

We've inherited our meaning of money from our parents, class or culture.

Expanding your value and possibilities

A certain mind-set about money can hold us back. If we think 'rich' is a dirty word, it will be more difficult to increase our funds. There's going to be a ceiling – a certain amount that we think is 'a lot of money' – where we unconsciously put the brakes on either charging more, earning more, investing more in ourselves or spending in a way that gives us joy. A place where we think 'that's too much to ask', lower our prices or walk away from the thing we really want.

This is not about ripping people off or getting into crippling debt. First things first – make money in a way that brings value to the world. If you don't know how you bring value, go back and read the section on work or have a think about changing what you do. Wallace D. Wattles puts it well in *The Science of Getting Rich*[31]: 'If you are selling any man anything which does not add more to his life than the thing he gives you in exchange, you can afford to stop it ... Give every man more in use value than you take from him in cost value; then you are adding to the life of the world by every business transaction.'

Once you are less shackled to the idea of earning or charging a lot as being somehow shameful, when you are sure of all the non-monetary value you provide through what you offer, you will feel freer to charge the true price for your service or product. If needs be, write a list of all the value you give or contribute to in exchange for the money you charge. For example, if you are a sports coach for children, the obvious value you provide is in teaching children how to play sport. But there might be other, secondary value, that you provide too – giving parents some time off babysitting, getting children into the fresh air and increasing their fitness, nurturing a love of exercise early and creating fond memories – it might be socializing with other children in a fun environment, or boosting confidence. All of these things are part of the service you offer.

> In order to boost your value when negotiating a salary or offering services, try stating a range, where the lowest point is what you actually want. One study by Columbia business school psychologists found that when job applicants stated a range as their requested salary (e.g. £50,000 to £70,000), where the lowest number was their desired pay packet, they received significantly higher salaries.[32]

Charge a price that feels scary to ask for. Too many of us undervalue our services in terms of money, then become resentful when we put in the time and effort necessary to do a good job to the standard we want to do it.

We need to provide value to others, to feel valuable to others – it gives us satisfaction and fulfilment as humans – but we struggle to ask for the money that would allow us to do this without becoming bitter. We're not good at accurately rating how much we should – and could – charge for our time and service. There's such a thing as being reassuringly expensive to a customer – allowing them to realize what they are purchasing has value, and that value is recognized by the person they are buying it from.

If you value yourself, and what you offer, you will also spend money investing in improving your offering, in growth, which supports other businesses and leads to progress all around. Because what you spend money on is a sign of what you value, investing it in yourself (wisely) is also an act that promotes your own well-being. There's a phrase – put your money where your mouth is – i.e. back up what you are saying with a tangible investment. I'd go one further: put your money where your heart is, or even where you want your heart to be. Spend your money the way someone who loves themselves, or values their life, would. If that means saving for a gym membership, then so be it.

One of the key things here is spending your money on new experiences – ones that promote inner progress. There's something called the hedonic treadmill, which informs this way of spending to promote happiness. Humans adapt very quickly, returning to a relatively stable level of happiness whatever the circumstances – good or bad. That means if you spend an awful lot of money on maintaining a very opulent lifestyle, after a while you will simply get used to it, and it will cease to bring you the contentment it used to. But if you cut down on the everyday spends, and use that money for new experiences, you'll feel more satisfied.

There's nothing wrong with wanting to be rich so that we can have more experiences in life. Earning money or spending money so that we increase the value of what we can offer the world is not 'greedy' or morally wrong. The problem comes when we make being rich a rigid 'must' or 'should' – that we *have to* earn lots of money. That's when we grip and grasp, getting competitive and scrambling for the goal at any cost. The other trap with accumulating wealth is when we want money to fill some other gap in our psyche that money is poorly suited to satisfy. This is important. If the reason you want a car is a sense of status and power, then you may find a car is not the best way to get that.

Your dream budget

See if you can expand your range for what is possible for you, to find out where you are limiting yourself with a belief that you cannot earn more, or that the world doesn't value you enough. Gaining money for money's own sake is the goal of a nincompoop. Instead, look at the things you want, in an ideal world; if money was no object. Then attach a price to them. It might look like this:

- *Less anxiety (therapy: £60 a week)*
- *More time off (buy holiday days from work: £300)*
- *Personal trainer (£60 a week)*
- *Massage training course (£400)*

The sky's the limit. It doesn't matter that you might be unable to afford these things right now – the important thing is to set a goal for where you want to go. Work out what your yearly income would need to be to afford all of these things. Then you can list what they would give you and others, too, if you were able to get them. For example, more time off means more relaxation, more time spent time with family, a greater sense of love/peace, more time spent with nature, perhaps; better relationships with friends and being more available at work when you are there. Sure, if you just want something because it looks pretty and it's fun, well leave it on. Just know that that is the reason you want it – and hey, maybe there are other ways to give yourself pretty, fun things in life – something you could give yourself now.

The very act of writing down what you want is a brilliant way to get in touch with yourself, and it may give you an impetus to move forward – something to fuel you to charge the uncomfortable price for your services, to look for opportunities to earn money, to ask for a rise. If looking at the budget feels overwhelming, then you may want to go back and write an intermediary list – one that doesn't seem too far off from where you are now but that stretches you.

In the meantime, there are some tangible advantages to be gained, should you find yourself in a position with not as much money as you would prefer. I don't want to go too Pollyanna on you or deny that losing/not having money is stressful, but there are ways to look at being – ahem – less abundant – so that you make the most of it.

Shoestring living

The primary benefit to having less money is that it is uncomfortable, which means you have to wake up. We live in a comfort-addicted, perfection-obsessed culture, asleep at the wheel as we bump from purchasing one numbing experience to another. We buy to get high – layering the exhilaration of a bargain, or a shiny new acquisition, over a difficult feeling, so we can ignore our inner discomfort.

When you have less money, you have the opportunity to be more aware of the world, simply because you can't afford to buy the same level of distraction. Being forced to sit with that, we learn it is more bearable than we thought. It might be challenging but we can live through it, and it can actually set us free to direct our lives how we want to move forward – rather than simply navigating ourselves away from pain.

By being exposed to your discomfort, you can learn how to work with what is, how to go into an experience fully and enjoy it for what's there, rather than buying things or trying to change it because it feels less-than-perfect. You have to look for what is right, rather than complain that the people are wrong or the venue is wrong or the clothes are wrong or the food is wrong.

The second benefit to being down on your money luck is the fact that having less automatically puts you in cooperation with other people. You might have to reach out to people: to either share experiences because it is cheaper, or to ask for help, or to propose doing something together. What is great about having less money is that you have to get creative. You have to be creative about having the fun you want. Can you work backstage in order to see the concert for free? Can you dog-sit or apartment/house-swap to get free accommodation on holiday? What do you have of value to sell? What do you have to exchange? What services can you provide for people? Basically, you have to up your hustle-game; challenge what you think is possible, challenge what other people think is possible from you and get as resourceful as you can. You may find you have more than you thought you did.

Having less money is not a prerequisite for waking up to either of these truths, but if you find yourself in hard times, it can focus your mind into such realization. Preferably, we'd all discover this with a decent amount of cash – but we don't, because the way we spend our money doesn't necessarily help us.

Getting conscious with money

There was a point in between jobs, where, I was, shall we say, skint. I was not bringing any money in, and I had deeply underestimated the rate I needed to spend it to live on my own in central London. The wake-up call for me was exchanging years-old foreign currency from Russia, Thailand and Europe to get enough money to buy groceries; and putting pots and pans on eBay to pay rent on time. I have more feathers to my bow than queuing at Western Union with a handful of coins ('I'm afraid, madam, that's actually a peso') and more to offer the world than hard-wearing crockery. Sure, prices in my city were high and the media, competitive, but if I looked within my circle of influence, I also wasn't paying attention to my finances enough.

I hate the idea of budgeting or 'saving' because it makes me think of sitting at home, eating a tin of baked beans (or some tuna in brine if I'm lucky), depriving myself of friends and fun. What I did come up with, with my coach at the time, was this idea of getting conscious around money. It wasn't necessarily about changing or cutting back; it was just about becoming more aware, without judgement, and then taking it from there. The thing is, when you discover you spent more than £50 on coffee one month, it's hard not to make a decision to slim down the cappuccino intake.

If you want to do this, too, go through last month's bank statement (there are also a number of apps that will help you track your purchases). Have an open, accepting mind – don't judge yourself for the past (or cry over spilt milk). You can feel proud of yourself for doing this.

Get out your highlighters and start grouping. Maybe you pick one colour for bills – as well as rent or mortgage, you might include other monthly outgoings like energy, mobile phone, internet, insurance, etc.

You could also underline and colour-coordinate transport, then food, then subscriptions (charities, Netflix, Spotify etc.). There will still be some things left over. Look at all the transactions over £20. (If you are a big spender, you might want to make this more.) Can you separate into groups? Perhaps going out, or health – massages, gym membership?

Once you've got these groupings, you begin to get a

clearer picture of where the money is going. Decide what you want to do about that. I realized I was haemorrhaging a lot of money on cheap taxis. I discussed it with my coach and we decided that I would set up a separate account into which I could put money when I chose to get the bus instead of a taxi – so I put the price of an Uber in the new bank account. It was far more rewarding to do it like that – it actually felt as though I was *earning* money, rather than cutting back. You can do this, too – putting the price of a latte in your savings account when you go past a coffee shop and don't buy one!

PURPOSE

Finding your purpose is a somewhat grandiose term. Endeavouring to answer the question, 'What's your purpose?' can feel like trying to catch a cloud. That's why a lot of us give up on the whole concept – where philosophers and prophets have fought and failed, why should we mere mortals be any more fruitful? And anyway – what's the point?

That's a very important question, actually: what's the point? Or, what's *our* point? As humans, and as individuals? There are many schools of thought about what, as humans, our purpose is. In many monotheistic religions (Christianity, Islam, Judaism) the reason for being is to worship God and to do his will – and that worship is expressed by living in accordance with what the scriptures of those religions advise (and that's where the arguments start again).

Buddhism teaches that the purpose of life is to end suffering. Nice one, but again, there are a few different suggestions about how to do that (apparently, even Buddhists aren't all of one mind on this topic). There are some who subscribe to the notion that it is our purpose to have children – to breed and sustain the human race. I'm not a big fan of that one because I have a womb and I'd rather it didn't all get too *Handmaid's Tale* anytime soon. Or perhaps it is love for all, or developing total compassion, which is our purpose. The quest for wisdom, truth and knowledge show up a lot as something from which we could derive purpose, as well as helping others and making the world a better place to live. Some rate physical pleasure high on the meaningful list – others say it is merely a distraction from achieving a greater state of consciousness: transcending our bodily urges. Nihilists say there is no purpose to life; it is essentially meaningless. Or that we have to create our own. I quite enjoy the boldly brutal stance of Chinese Legalism on the matter, which states it is meaningless to even look for meaning in human existence and all activity should be directed towards increasing the power of the ruler and wealth of the state. Happy days.

When I'm talking about purpose, I'm talking about what gives you meaning in life. I'm talking about why you think you are here on this earth and what you are choosing to spend that time doing. But why care at all? Especially if evolution means we are just randomly plonked here by chance.

Well, it seems that there is scientific evidence that shows we do care: having purpose is good for our health. Eudemonic happiness (a type of happiness linked to meaning, rather than simply pleasure) was linked to lower levels of inflammatory gene expression and higher levels of antibody and antiviral genes. A large study in the *Lancet*[33] found that a sense of purpose and meaning was linked to a longer life. Purpose in life is linked to cognitive function – especially as we age. Additionally, people who believe there is meaning to life sleep better.[34]

But if random evolution means we are only here by accident, then aren't we searching for something that doesn't exist? Possibly – it depends how you think about it. If you are just here by accident, think about how remarkable that is. It's pretty extraordinary. Perhaps your purpose, then, is to really inhabit this body that you accidentally adopted, to really be here as much as possible – as alive and incarnate as you can on this physical earth – whatever making the most of a chance occurrence looks like to you. You might win the Lottery simply because of the luck of the draw, but that doesn't mean that you should spend the money like it is has no value.

Having purpose, to me, means living a meaningful life, an existence filled to the brim with value – you find value in what you do and experience, you feel you are valuable, you are in touch with what you value in others, and you act in accordance with that which you value. We all have days when we don't feel like that sometimes, when we feel like hiding under a blanket with a dog or a cat or a cheesecake or all three, but that's the intention.

And intention it is. Finding purpose is not the same as

achievement, although it may express itself along the way as accomplishing certain things. Achieving is about doing things. Purpose is more of a way of being. The word comes from the twelfth-century Old French '*porpos*', meaning 'aim or intention', and further back from the Latin root of '*por*', meaning 'forth'. I think of purpose as the way we move forward – how we go forth. Purpose is a kind of energetic navigation – it decides the way we're pointing and provides the drive to take the first step. I think of purpose as being a kind of North Star on steroids.

If you're aware that you don't have a sense of meaning, it can feel disorientating. You may feel restless a lot, or as though you're just drifting from one project to another, with no idea why you are doing what you are doing and feeling bad about that. Even when you are moving in a certain direction, you may feel as though you're just going through the motions, for no real reason that moves you, other than that you have no idea what else to do, or that the other options look worse. You don't feel depressed as such, but there's this low-level dissatisfaction about your life that nags at you whenever you stop what you're doing long enough to notice it. You might mask it in busyness, to prevent the feeling from arising. When you don't have a sense of purpose, then comfort becomes your top priority and any sort of suffering and challenge is to be avoided, as it feels pointless.

Some people get very anxious about finding their purpose, for some or all of these reasons. They feel they must live up to their full potential – anything less than that is a waste of their life – and that having a purpose looks a certain way, or that a person with purpose is successful in all the ways we sometimes value success in this world. For me, purpose is about learning to be as much yourself as possible – and sometimes that's not a case of doing, but of letting go of all the things that aren't yours. Some clients come to me for coaching to help them find their purpose and talk about it as some sort of macho intrepid mission. It's not about toughening up and pushing through, but about slowing down and being willing to let go.

See, uncovering what is meaningful for us and acting in accordance with that is more like learning a vulnerable art of undressing, except instead of peeling off our clothes we're removing all the dirt and sludge we've become smothered in over the years, some of which was thrown at us, some of which we fell into by accident, and some of which we grabbed willingly to protect our precious little inner being inside.

In Jamie Catto's book, *Insanely Gifted*, he tells a story of the artistic process of becoming and giving from another perspective: 'When they asked Michelangelo about his famous David sculpture he said that as soon as they brought him the huge slab of rock he could see the figure of David standing there within. His job was just to chip away the excess marble …'[35]

Finding purpose is mostly a process of de-armouring, lifting off our outdated protections, so that we can rediscover the beauty we have inside us, and let it shine out and share it with the world. Then we can breathe more easily, hear more clearly and feel more precisely, and it's easier to get in touch with that voice we haven't been able to hear over all the outside conditioning, the work directives, the media, the family messages, the angry exes, the fear, the shoulds, the shouldn'ts, the have-tos and the musts. Deep down, we all know what the next right step is at any one time. It's just that the way we've been living our lives means we can't hear the voice that tells us any more. Somewhere, years ago, we ignored it, because it told us to do something inconvenient, difficult or painful and we silenced it and repressed it until it got so quiet we have no idea what it sounds like any more. You know the voice – it sometimes tells us, 'I want to go now', or, 'I like that, give me more of that', or, 'That hurts now, no more'. It's the one that sometimes says, 'I really want to kiss him', or, 'Cancel it, I don't want to do it', or, 'Go this way', even when the way it points is dark and scary and you have no idea where it leads.

Sometimes, what feels like our purpose clashes with what our parents wanted for us or the sort of thing we feel we should do. Maybe we've spent years studying to be an architect, only to find we love watercolours. Or we've bought a beautiful home and have a wonderful family, but our heart wants to travel. We can't see how to move forward, without breaking other people's hearts or our own. It can be agonizing, but the only thing to do is surrender and admit to yourself that you hear the voice and you are willing to follow it, even if you can't see what to do right now.

There's a beautiful bit in Mark Nepo's *The Little Book of*

Awakening[36] where he tells the story of his friend Robert, who was carrying gallons of red paint into his house after mixing it outside, brush in his mouth, cloth under his arm. He didn't want to put it down to open the door and so did an awkward shuffle and almost went inside. 'I lost my grip, stumbled backward and wound up on the ground, red gallons all over me', Robert tells Nepo.

This incident makes Nepo muse on how we all do something similar in life, not with paint, but with our emotional baggage and the stories we carry about our past or our future, or even ourselves. Sometimes in order to move through the next door, to take advantage of the openings that appear in our lives, we have to let things go. We have to put down what we are carrying, if we want to cross the threshold. Finding your purpose can be a bit like that. A case of removing all that you are holding on to that isn't really part of you, so you not only know which door is the right one to open, but can make your way through it.

We'll have lots of doors to choose from, and they might be the right door one day, and the wrong door the next. To talk about finding your life purpose is a bit of a misnomer. It suggests that you can only have one purpose and if you're not 100 per cent sure what it is, well then, you're wasting your precious time here on earth, until you find it out and devote your life to it. In my opinion, you can have lots of different purposes – your job is only to find what gives you purpose, or the direction you should move in, right now. That's as much as you can ever know. We're all constantly changing and adapting. Let's not shackle our souls to any one thing for the rest of our lives just because it's a Sunday afternoon and we're in the grip of a wee existential panic about not being worthwhile or having a bit of a raggedy CV.

For me, purpose is not something that arrives from outside but is more a question of what your relationship to yourself and the wider world is at any one time. It changes with you, it's fluid and there can/should be no pain in that, because every lesson is valuable. Living with purpose is a way of relating to your experiences, so that moving through pain and discomfort is worthwhile, rather than something to be avoided, because you can use what you've learnt to help others in the same situation. If you can face your challenges consciously and work out how to get through them – on your own or with the help of others – then when someone else like you (for there are many) comes up against the same struggle, you can lead the way for them. This is how we can approach pain, grief and hurt lovingly.

I've learnt that 'being in your purpose' or 'living your purpose' – to use somewhat grandiose terminology – is really just a matter of answering yes to at least two of these three things at any one time. The first is around learning: are you growing or stretching yourself in some way? Are you progressing? The second is around enjoyment, or feelings: do you find your life satisfying? Is it fulfilling? The third is about your relationship to others and the wider world: are you able to share what you are learning? Are you helping others? Psychiatrist David Viscott wrote in his book *Finding Your Strength in Difficult Times: A Book of Meditations*: 'The purpose of life is to discover your gift.. The work of life is to develop it. The meaning of life is to give your gift away.'[37]

Help! I can't hear my inner voice

Suggesting 'tuning into your inner voice' is deeply unhelpful advice for anyone experiencing a 'beige spot' in their lives. Beige and foggy and a bit irritated was how I felt when people spoke to me about inspiration and finding purpose when I worked in a dark newsroom with anxiety-inducing targets all day. 'I'll find my goddamn purpose when I have time,' I grumbled inwardly.

If you feel the same, I have one piece of advice for you. Slow down. Delegate. Start saying no. Plan nothingness. Hours in your week where you don't do things, you just get there and then decide how you feel. In the morning, at lunchtime, after work, ask yourself: 'How do I feel? and 'What does my body want right now?'

Slowing down will be uncomfortable; because you've been racing at that speed for so long, it's unnerving to change velocity. There's a sailing term, 'land sickness', which relates to when you are on board a boat for days, and the weather's rough but your sea legs are sturdy; people might be puking over the side, but you've got this, no problem (damn landlubbers). Then you anchor up, or come ashore, walk off the boat and, oh, dear Lord, that's when the motion sickness kicks in. You have to take seasickness tablets to stop the nausea of returning to stability.

This happens when we slow down sometimes. It feels bad. We might blame slowing down for being the problem, but really it's the disruptive motion of our old lives that's still in our bodily rhythms.

Plus, when we slow down we begin to feel all the not-so-nice things we hadn't felt because of the distracting motion in our old lives – anger, or grief, or loneliness. Being misunderstood or hurt. Give yourself full approval for where you are. Accept that feeling such pain is part of getting rid of it. It helps. It's a bit like a hangover. One of the reasons you feel so rubbish is because, to process the alcohol, the liver initially has to convert the alcohol into something called acetaldehyde, which is joyfully toxic, and so you get a whole bunch of crappy symptoms like sweating, nausea and vomiting. It means the alcohol is leaving your system and you're on your way to feeling better, but wow, it can feel rough.

Once you're in that slower space, and the fog is clearing, it's possible to start taking a better look at who you are, and how you might want to engage with the world. But first, simply send yourself a bit of love and gratitude, because asking: 'What am I here on earth for? What can I do?' is a beautifully awake and alert question, bursting with humanity.

Aside from slowing down, there are a few other things you can try to help point you in the right direction:

- *Write down all the skills you think you have.*
- *Then ask a friend: 'If you were going to come for me for help on one thing, what would it be?' Or ask: 'If you were going to recommend me to someone for something, what would it be?' (Another question you could ask is: 'What do you appreciate about me?' This can also show you what you have to offer.)*
- *Next, write down all the difficult things you have gone through. This is a list you may be able to use to empathize with others and support them through their own difficult things. How could you help other people in the same situation?*
- *Think about things that you find fulfilling. List them. If there aren't many, think about some things that you want to try.*

Sit with this new knowledge of where you already provide meaning and how you could provide more. Don't get hung up on it, but simply commit to being curious, and slowing down enough to follow what feels right.

YOUR WORLDVIEW

Deep below the surface of our being – in that ocean of dreams, memories and buried feelings – there abides a patient captain, sitting at the bridge of a submarine.

We don't always know she's there, apart from when the vessel is moved, maybe by music, a baby laughing, a beautiful landscape or by a marriage ceremony.

Sometimes the waters are rocked by more painful vibrations – when we witness disasters on the news, when we lose a loved one, when we fail, or watch others crumple through the same disappointment; times we are betrayed and in the freedom of forgiveness.

At such moments, we sense movement under the waters: the captain has called the crew into action, the propellers judder into life, and suddenly we realize there may be something else that can power our thoughts, feelings and behaviour other than bold rationality, the hustling to-do list, the routine triumphs and mundane irritants that dominate our daily life.

We may not be able to identify or label what is stirred ... but we know it in a mystical sense: that there is something deep and strong and pure moving within us, and it has us cast around with fresh eyes, as if we've peeled back a film from our existence, and are being asked to engage with something more true – those big questions, questions we don't often ask and sometimes completely refuse to. I think there are five big ones:

1. *What is the nature of humanity – are we good or bad or neither?*
2. *Why is there so much suffering?*
3. *What is our relationship to the universe – and this planet?*

4. What happens after we die?
5. What is love?

These questions are so vital and the answers so unverifiable, they often scare us. They require us to trust in our felt sense as humans, not in our names or our degree results, our salaries or our looks. Sometimes, the very prospect of engaging with this is too much, so we refuse to acknowledge these moments at all, afraid that the movement in the waters will persist and grow, until our very ocean floor trembles with a power that cannot be ignored. Yet, calmly, gently, persistently and in a deafening whisper, these questions ask us to upend our lives. To think differently, feel differently, act differently. It points our existence in an entirely different direction.

This subterranean navigation system is our worldview, and the captain guides us based on our beliefs. She is the most powerful commander of our souls and yet is completely surrendered to us, too, and waits patiently to see whether we will heed the call to engage with the invisible waters beneath us as they move. If we do, we can experience moments of joy and of pain and move forward in a way that best honours ourselves and the world.

When we don't, when we choose numbness over feeling, we can't access those spiritual moments of truth. Deaf and drowsy, we choose to live on the choppy surface, tossed around by wave after wave of superficial distractions. We can spend years, whole lifetimes, ignorant of these depths, and our captain, sad but devoted, sits on the bridge, waiting for us to wake up, as we waft through life, rudderless and restless, searching the horizon for something to direct us from the outside, rather than from within.

However, just because we don't examine these guiding beliefs, doesn't mean the submariner goes to sleep. Our worldview doesn't stop influencing our thoughts, feelings and behaviour. Ignorant of the depths, however, our worldview gets hijacked by the everyday – the school bully, the abusive comment on Instagram, the angry manager, the cheating spouse; by rejection, by prejudice, by cultural conformity, by religious dogma.

We allow the world to shape us, rather than us shaping our world. When that happens, certain beliefs can hold us back, trapping us in a view of self and other that strangles life's infinite possibilities before we even realize what they could be.

I'm using 'worldview' to mean beliefs about the world, in particular the things we can't see; the as-yet-unknown or the unknowable. It's what philosophers call the metaphysical. This both influences, and is influenced by, our relationship to the world, yet often it's so automatic, we don't consider what's powering it – and by association, steering us.

Believe it, then you'll see it

The first thing you have to do is believe in the power of belief. Believe that it can change your world. At the very least, be willing *to suspend your doubt* in the power of belief. Just for this section, banish from your mind the phrase 'I'll believe it when I see it'. It's the silliest phrase ever. Believe it, *then* you'll see it. That's the way the world works, most of the time. And it's why our beliefs about the world are so important.

Our beliefs are paintbrushes and pencils that draw and colour the landscape in front of us. They decide the topography of our reality. What we believe about adversity can transform the challenges we face in life, from a barefoot slog over the volcanic plains of Mordor to a sweaty but enjoyable hike through Elysium.

If we have a hopeful view of humanity, we can become agile climbers rather than static spectators. Whether we see the back of the traveller in front of us or the stars in the sky, depends on how far we can see. Whether we see the world as a battlefield strewn with bloodied bodies, or as dominated by oceans covering its surface, washing us all clean, depends on whether we are zooming in or zooming out. How we see trees changes whether we hug them or chop them down, whether we plant or consume.

So what makes for a helpful belief versus an unhelpful one? It seems the first attribute is making sure that your belief is flexible and acknowledges a changing, adapting world. That means believing, like the Ancient Greek philosopher Heraclitus did, in flux: people can change, physical circumstances change and emotional states can change. It's also helpful to have a flexible relationship with your beliefs (being open-minded) and to ensure that flexibility is inbuilt to them (thinking that the world must or should be a certain way is unhelpfully rigid).

Believing that people can change and improve actually helps them change and improve, according to research done by Stanford University psychologist Carole Dweck. She proposed the 'growth mind-set' theory, which has been pivotal in changing the way we think about education and attainment.

As part of a series of experiments, she identified two main types of belief that even younger children have about their intelligence. There's the 'fixed mind-set', which, for example, is when you believe that intelligence is something you are born with, and all you can do is uncover this innate gift. If you have a malleable view, you believe you can improve your intelligence and change. Her research[38] showed that children with fixed theories about their intelligence struggled to improve their performance over the school year – and this was the case just as much for children with high IQs, who were praised for being bright. When these kids experienced failure, they saw it as a sign that they had reached the limits of what they were good at – it wasn't something they could change, but a personal failing that couldn't be improved upon. This meant that not only were they much more adversely affected by it, but they didn't make as much effort attempting to learn anything to improve their skills.

Dweck's research found that children were similarly impacted on by fixed beliefs about their personalities. If a child with a fixed view of their personality was rejected by one clique in a schoolyard, they moved away and stopped trying to make new friends – even if there were ten other groups ready to welcome them. Because these children thought the problem was in them, they viewed this as evidence of something they couldn't do anything about. The difficulty with this is if children retreat when they are rejected, they don't learn social skills and so their belief that they are fundamentally unlikeable ends up seeming real.

A belief that our natures are fundamentally fixed affects, adults too. Another study showed that if white people think racism is a fixed attribute – innate and unchangeable – they are likely to exhibit prejudiced behaviour even if they aren't actually prejudiced. This would exhibit itself in not even wanting to engage in activities like learning about African-American history. The psychologists conducting the study suggested that despite not having racist beliefs, the white participants were worried about uncovering something they could not change, and so they avoided situations with black people where their fears might be confirmed and were more resistant, also, to activities that might reduce prejudice.

Another of Dweck's studies had college students fill in a questionnaire which ascertained whether they had fixed or malleable beliefs. When the students with fixed personalities experienced low moods, they were much less able to cope than those with more malleable beliefs about themselves, whose ability to cope was actually boosted by such moments, which encouraged them to build new skills, problem solve, and seek out different ways of thinking or feeling.[39]

Whether or not we believe we can cope with adversity actually affects whether or not we can cope with adversity.

This is the premise of a type of psychological therapy called REBT (Rational Emotive Behaviour Therapy) and it's based on the idea that it's not the event that causes psychological disturbance in people, but the irrational and unhelpful beliefs that are triggered by them. Albert Ellis, who developed the system, was influenced by Epictetus in the *Enchiridion*, who wrote: 'Men are disturbed not by things, but by the views which they take of them.'

If we believe we are ever-expanding human beings who can cope, learn and improve – if we see our challenges as difficult but not impossible, then everything seems that little bit brighter, and we carry a candle of hope with us, even when it gets dark. This expansive attitude means that we are able to seek out those things that will help us to improve. Mountains are not there to show us how small we are but to teach us how to climb.

This last bit is crucial and is where a lot of positive thinkers go awry, in my humble opinion. Believing you can overcome your low mood doesn't, automatically, mean that your mood will magically improve. What it means is that you've created an opportunity to look at and look for ways to improve your mood, and you may find some (a caveat to this is that it is not a stick to beat yourself over the head with when you're struggling to feel better).

Ser vs Estar

In Spanish there are two words meaning to be: **ser** and **estar** – but they mean slightly different things. One is permanent (**ser**) and one is temporary (**estar**). We might be fat right now, but we're not fat – it's just a temporary condition. We might be anxious right now, but we aren't anxious people. That isn't actually us. 'Right now' is your best friend when it comes to putting things in perspective: You don't know what to do right now, you don't know how you feel about this right now, you're scared right now. Things change, and so will you and your feelings.

Believing that you will be good at astrophysics doesn't make you good at astrophysics, but if you want to become an astrophysicist and trust that you have the capacity, then you will need to find a teacher, and do the things that someone who wanted to learn astrophysics would do, rather than stay in the same old job, doing the same old thing.

Belief, in this sense, is not an instruction manual, but a pair of glasses that lets you read the instruction manual better, or see that there's been one in the box the whole time.

Pain, adversity, humanity

My experience of adversity (also known by other aliases – suffering, pain, despair, disaster, sickness, anxiety, distress, misery) has been powerfully altered over the last two years. It's not made life any less painful or turbulent. In twelve months, I quit my job, started a business, lost two grandparents, suffered from periods of depression, and saw a friend die by suicide. At times, it has felt excruciating – but somehow my beliefs about pain, struggle and our capacity as humans to transcend and be transformed by adversity have shifted me to a place where I can *feel* them but they don't break me. Some of these painful experiences did see bits of my life change – but these bits were already broken. Some of them saw whole chunks of me fall off – the workaholic, the heavy drinker, the sarcastic one, the busy one; but those bits of me needed to go. I'm not a chemist, and I'm not heavily religious, but there's a helpful metaphor in the Bible that draws on both disciplines. It's repeated a lot, but the basic principle is most obviously stated in Isaiah 48.10 when God says, 'Behold, I have refined you, but not as silver; I have tried you in the furnace of affliction.'

Gold gets harder and stronger when it's heated to high temperatures. When silver is heated, it separates from any impurities. In this way, painful experiences can help show you more of what is true, if you let them. Suffering is the place you find and develop compassion for others. It's a horrible, cosmic joke, but being terrified is the only place you can discover or develop courage. Being hurt or wounded is the only way you'll have an opportunity to let go or forgive. It's easy to be a good person when everything is wonderful, but it's powerful to be a good person when the chips are down.

When melons are under stressful climate conditions, there is an increase in sugar, as they try and survive, and they end up being much more delicious. Heatwaves cause higher rates of photosynthesis in peaches, which means the sugar levels increase in the fruit. Peaches ripen earlier and are extra sweet when things get hot.

I like the word adversity to describe pain or suffering, because the thing about adversity is that you meet it and face it. Adversity has a curious etymology – it actually originally comes from the Latin word '*advertere*', meaning to 'turn towards', 'to face' or 'to confront', as if the instructions for how to handle adversity were contained within the word itself. We turn towards the pain, and that is the only way we can know how to overcome it.

Adversity is the place that teaches you skills to be a better human. Maybe you can empathize with and help someone else who finds themselves in a hole and thinks they're the first one to land there. They'll have to climb the ladder on their own, but you can at least direct them to where the ladder is, so that they know they are not alone and that there is a way out.

When it feels too much, just know that the world is always changing. Have you ever tried to string out a good feeling or grip on to happiness forever? Yup, you can't, as anyone who has ever attempted to go on a day-long date will know. The same is true of pain. It doesn't burn with the same intensity forever. Something good will come of it if you sit with it and allow it to soften your heart. Something good will come of it if you make sure it does.

Reality check

A note here, because I think this is all well and good to say when you're not half drowning in the eye of a hideous whirlpool of suffering. When you are, it's just sobbing into your pillow, wailing, 'I'm learning nothing, there is no point to this, it's just awful, life is terrible.'

A silly example of this (that did not feel silly at all at the time) is when I was panicking one day about a story deadline and my friend, also replete with precious-metal metaphors, told me, 'Diamonds are formed under pressure.'

I looked at her, my eyes fizzing from lack of sleep and five coffees before 9 a.m., my tongue furry and feral, and replied somewhat sarcastically, 'Are they actually? Because right now I'm just experiencing extreme anxiety.'

What I did learn that day, however, after reaching diamond-forming-point (my computer decided to install all its updates in a two-hour reboot and I burst into tears on the phone to a friend), is that I needed to be a bit nicer to myself. When lessons aren't coming, and you're still in pain, just pour a bit of love over yourself. Cancel the things you don't need to do. Call a friend. Breathe in and breathe out, with one hand on your heart and one hand on your belly. Stroke a dog/cat/

tree/partner. Get into nature. Do the things that soothe you.

Be kind to your sweet, lovely self. Everything will do as it will do. There are some kinds of suffering that call for learning, conquering, being brave, opening up and being vulnerable. Other times, and actually if I'm honest, at all times, the moment calls for us to be tender, caring and loving to ourselves.

If all else fails, see if you can find some laughter. This one time I had a spell of terrible depression and couldn't leave the house. I ordered a weird combination of food to my door and half-heartedly ate it before leaving it by the bed. Then my friend came over to see me and, getting up to go to the door, I put my bare foot in a whole load of sweet-and-sour chicken and burst into tears. I opened the door sobbing and my friend was desperately asking, 'What's wrong?' I pointed to all the sauce on my foot and wailed that I had stepped in food, and she sort of looked at it in horror and then looked at me, with a kind of 'I don't know what the right thing to say about this is' expression, and came up with, 'It could be quite moisturizing.'

This attempt at consolation was so weird and untrue and useless that I just said, 'It's not.' And then we both began to laugh.

Zoom in and out

Playing with perspective is one way to shift your worldview so that it helps you navigate your feelings and behaviour better. I think of it as zooming in, or zooming out. Are you looking at one small part of life or are you looking at the whole? Which is most helpful?

For example, a series of terrible events can happen, and it can fracture our view of the world, if we zoom in and focus just on this. But if we expand our worldview, and if we open our hearts to seeing the good things, too, then often it can feel a little less painful.

Mark Nepo relates a parable in his *The Little Book of Awakening*. It's about a Hindu master who, fed up with his complaining apprentice, decides to teach him a lesson:

The Hindu master asks his apprentice to put a handful of salt into a glass of water and drink it. As the apprentice spits it out, the master asks, 'How does it taste?'

To which the young man replies, 'Bitter.'

The two of them then walk to the nearby lake, where the Hindu master asks the apprentice to put another handful of salt in. He then instructs him to take a cup and drink from the lake. 'How does it taste now?' he asks his young charge.

'Fresh,' the apprentice replies.

The moral of the story (health and safety concerns aside) is that our pain will feel as concentrated as the container it is held in. It's not really about getting rid of pain – pain in life is there and will always be there. Nepo writes: 'So when you are in pain, the only thing you can do is to enlarge your sense of things. Stop being a glass. Become a lake.'

Becoming a lake begins for me by realizing, when I'm down or feeling stressed, that there is someone in the world feeling just like me right now. Probably even within a fifty-mile radius, someone a bit like me, going through the exact same thing, having the exact same feelings.

Expanding my world means looking at old things. I live in London and I like looking at historic buildings. When I look at St Paul's, I think it's so beautiful and inspiring: how the architect and everyone else came together to make it for us all are now just dirt and bones and old reported bits of history. And how someone else is going to come along, and have the same semi-profound thought, when this building is still standing and I am dead.

Zooming out means pausing for fifteen seconds and looking at the sky, and the clouds going past, and knowing that I have no control over them. I let my smallness soothe me, and feel hopeful, knowing that there's so much I don't know and that maybe it will all be okay, and that if it's not there's very little I can do about it, other than surrender to that sense of mystery, and dream big.

At other times, it's helpful for me to zoom in, to focus solely on what is in front of my face, what I can see, hear, and touch physically. I remember that one time I had a huge project to complete, and halfway through, I felt exhausted, I just couldn't see how I would ever get it done. That was a time when I zoomed in, and simply focused on what I had to do in the next hour, and then the next day, and then the next month.

Ernest Hemingway has great advice for writers: 'All you have to do is write one true sentence. Write the truest sentence that you know.' There's something about doing this that feels possible. And once you do that possible thing, you look back and think, 'Okay, I did that one; maybe I can do the next one.'

One breath at a time. One step at a time. One self-loving thought at a time. Just looking at what's in front of you. Then repeating that process until, somewhere along the way, you realize you've travelled a little further than you thought you could, and you begin to believe.

Love, death, pain, humanity and God

What you come to believe about the world from the experiences and emotions that stir your own inner submariner are unique to you. We all have our own worldview – it's about becoming actively conscious of yours, so that you aren't navigating blind. I've also suggested some methods for setting your compass in order that it functions more effectively for you – being flexible with your beliefs, knowing that both circumstances and you can change, not seeing pain as a punishment, more as an opportunity for growth – zooming in and zooming out when you need some space to breathe and a more helpful perspective.

As for my own beliefs? Well, here's how I see it.

> *Death:* This is how we change form. Matter can't be destroyed. Things only ever change state.
> *Love:* This is how much power we have.
> *Pain:* This is how we learn courage, compassion and acceptance.

Humanity: The only thing we need to believe in is our capacity for change.

God/higher power: This is what teaches you how to let go with love. To surrender to what is and to simply trust. It is the relationship to all four combined, but more than that: to hope, goodness and the best you can imagine. The relationship to a higher power comes before everything else.

PLUGGING INTO THE BIGGER PICTURE

Care about the world. You need it and it needs you. Your invitation is this – to care for and value your own life so that you can care for and value the life of the planet. To treat the lives of others with loving kindness and be constantly reminded to be sweet and gentle with yourself, too, because we all share in and are made of the same magic.

At first, caring in this way might feel a bit juddery – a stop-start process as you fill up your energy pot (take care of yourself) and pour out from it (offer to others). As you relax a bit more, you'll see it's more about letting yourself be a sieve. If you can trust enough to open yourself up and expand your perspective to a greater vision, you'll be able to let more of the world in to nourish you (it really wants to). The 'filling up' process becomes automatic (joy is everywhere, waiting to refresh us) and you'll never get to the bottom of your resources, or need to stop and seek for ways to fill up your pot, to grasp for energy unhelpfully or unhealthily, using the world or people instead of experiencing them.

You won't have to expend effort as you pour it out either, but rather can just continually let the natural flow happen. It doesn't require you to do or control; it just requires you to listen to the bigger thing, realize that you're part of it and allow your caring to be plugged into that.

It's about seeing the joy that's present and available to us when we open our eyes to the wider world; and sweeping away anything in the way. Sometimes you might be able to do this by meeting your obstacle with a smile and open heart. Other times, the impediments in our path will only dissolve through tears. It doesn't matter whether suffering or good fortune is your route; both are part of living. Just know that peace and joy lie underneath everything. There's more of it than you could imagine. So much so that, once you've found it, you'll want to share it with everyone.

It doesn't mean sacrificing your life

I've been talking about giving a f**k about causes, projects, purpose, service; these are all grand words, but whatever you care about doesn't need to be impressive in any historical sense. What I really mean is: care about something that society, self-reliance or compliance doesn't 'require' you to. Something of your own choosing, that arises from a desire within. It can be litter picking, teaching, singing, cooking, writing, nursing, dancing. It doesn't have to be curing world hunger or malaria. In fact, get the idea of 'cure' out of your head completely.

The world doesn't need saving and neither do you. We've just been a little bit dozy, blurry-eyed and forgetful, that's all. Unfortunately, like anyone who has slept past their alarm, there's a tendency for us, upon waking up, to look around and panic. No time to enjoy a coffee or a croissant, because we're very late, and there's a lot to do. We look at that world in this urgent headspace and think, 'Oh God, there's mess and pain everywhere and there's so much to do and we must do it all ourselves and it's terrible and let's just throw ourselves into any activity at all, because everything is broken and desperately needs to be fixed.'

There are lots of people who will tell you this. Some will be sales people, who in the main are faking this attitude. Others will be politicians, some of whom are also excellent actors, and some of whom are genuinely sincere in their belief that action must be taken NOW and with a spirit of urgency and everyone is needed. There will be very well-meaning people who work for charities, who are totally earnest and are ready to sacrifice their lives for a cause. All these people and more will tell you how desperately important their thing is. Journalists, in particular, are a big fan of this. Ooh, and religious leaders. People with petitions. All in all, this merry band of vocational issue-junkies will impress upon you with utmost emergency how deeply they need you to do a certain thing or another. How time is running out. They are not quite wrong, but they aren't right either. And they do themselves a disservice with their seriousness. They besmirch the good name of caring. Give and help if you want to, but do not get sucked into this facsimile of caring for things you know aren't that important to you deep down. Listen to your submariner first, then decide on all other extraneous chatter. Also – nothing comes at any cost.

No cause is worth sacrificing your precious life for; for taking your attention off the whole, the bigger picture, and zooming in to channel all your energy into one thing, to the exclusion of all others. I'm not just referring to dramatic religious martyrdom. We forfeit our existence in many dull and dreary ways: decades in a job we hate, climbing a career ladder, mindlessly devoting ourselves to some vague sense of duty, paying off the mortgage, pouring all our energy into a relationship or raising a family. Quite often we dress the dishonourable devaluation of our own life in a cloak of virtue, wantonly wasting precious energy in support of some campaign, movement, political party or charity.

In the short term, this can be a way of hiding from ourselves. In the long term, it's a form of abandoning the intrinsic value of our own life. It's ignorant – it's almost as if we are trying to prove the worthiness of our existence when we're already here, already existing, already enough. It's arrogant – as if there is something we could do with our heads or our hands that could in any way match how breathtakingly special it is that we happen to be alive.

We can commit to projects, become engaged and absorbed in a cause or a certain subject of interest, but when what you're *doing* becomes more important than how you are *being*, take a deep breath and come back to yourself. This is it, and it's spectacular in its simplicity. You can sit here and contemplate yourself and your amazing body; it's wonderful to simply be. Let your shoulders sink down. Feel the space in your chest expand. Let your jaw soften, and the skin settle around your eyes. Feel the movements and rhythms in your body. See if you can notice any emotions. Look around you. The experience of this innate magic we have inside us, which comes from a bigger source, is your 'why', not some nebulous striving to defeat the bad. If defeating evil is our purpose, then we'll just continue to make more evil, because otherwise we'll run out of meaning.

Whole-y f★★k

Sometimes, instead of the 'what' – the bigger vision – we get stuck on the 'how'. This is getting distracted by logistics – which pose their own problem, don't get me wrong – but mechanics is actually just a lot of small things; it's not *the* big thing. It's possibly not even a thing at all, just a way of thinking. When I'm talking about plugging into something bigger, I'm talking about the whole world, the universe even. It's hard for us to think this way, especially if we are from a Western background. We really like to boil down things into their constituent parts, considering the whole as simply what you get accidentally when everything comes together, rather than adopting a more holistic view, as some of the East Asian philosophies do.

This fragmented way of thinking informs our everyday

– in fact it is so pervasive it can even affect how we look at images, which one study set out to prove. Researchers took American and Chinese students and showed them images – for example, a picture of a tiger in the forest – and then tracked their eye movements. American students tended to focus more on the central object, whereas the Chinese-born students looked more around the whole picture, taking in the context.[40]

Theoretical physicist David Bohm, a contemporary of Albert Einstein's, was led by his research in quantum mechanics to propose that the nature of reality was actually a coherent whole – not just a collection of parts. That at a subatomic level, everything is highly connected – more than most of us can even imagine. He believed that many of the world's divisions could be healed if we were to adjust our way of thinking towards a reality that is unbroken, coherent, harmonious. It's our fragmented way of thinking that makes us see the world as fragmented.[41]

It can boggle the mind a bit to imagine everything in the universe, ourselves included, overlapping and influencing each other, electrons knocking and boinging together, and everyone and everything so highly interconnected that the butterfly effect seems boring. We live in time, which means we like things orderly and linear, and we're used to separating things out to make sense of them, dividing them into mine and yours. That can be a useful way of operating. But that's all it is.

When I'm talking about plugging into something bigger,

I'm not saying care about communities or the planet because these things are superior to you or that you are small and inconsequential. The opposite, in fact. I'm saying: plug into this whole, this view of totality, and realize that the world would be incomplete without you and you would be incomplete without the world. Sometimes, realizing we are part of something greater (as well as acknowledging that we are also complete in our right), we can also remember our own greatness. Seeing our life, not only as a wonderful whole in and of itself, but also as part of a bigger whole, works as a reminder of who we really are, helping us to become and embody that. If this sounds spiritual, then you might be onto something. The etymology of the word 'holy' comes from the word 'whole'.

Don't do it to get it; do it to become it

It's good to give a f★★k, to want to make an impact on the world, but make sure it's about changing, and not about being the agent of that change.

Making things better for the world of which you are a part, helping life on a planet that enables you to live, rooted in a belief that you are connected and part of a whole, is sustaining and nourishing.

Caring about creating something life-affirming is almost impossible if you make it *your* mission. You're separating yourself from others and the planet. Your ego will get in the way of what's needed to complete it, and in the meantime you risk not going about it in a way that's affirming to your life.

Making it personal means deadlines. We don't have very long on this planet, especially if we want to bask in the credit, too. How terrible would it be if it's ★your★ project and you die before it's completed? Then your life will have come to nothing. You'll either have to rush and get anxious or make your project smaller. Much smaller, for you are less likely to ask for help, to collaborate, and you'll push for credit over your creation.

Dedication will be hard – if you're doing it just for your own ego, then when times get tough, those self-interested voices will shout louder. The comfort addiction will kick in. However, if you are answering to something bigger, it will be easier to take a break, be kind, and then find the strength, the inspiration, to carry on. Let the reason, the very thing you are working for, refuel you, not self-congratulation or the glory you may never win.

We want to be creating batons to pass on, not striving for completion. The goal is not the thing you want, anyway. Think about climbing a mountain: it's not actually about getting to the top – not really – because what do you do once you've reached the summit? Climb back down again.

It's about who you become in the process of climbing that mountain. The levels of fitness you have to achieve. The money you have to raise. The friends you make. The new skills you have to learn. The dedication you need to commit to. The fear you have to overcome. The countries you travel to. The beautiful landscape you see. The differences you encounter. The pain you overcome. The sickness. The exhilaration. The dark nights and the bright mornings. The wondering why you signed up to do this in the first place, and carrying on anyway. Getting to the top: well, that's just something to tell people back home.

Giving a f★★k means being engaged, interested and active both in life and in all that enables you to live. It's not actually about getting anywhere, though no doubt you'll find yourself in some interesting spots along the way, and achieving great things, if you're doing it right. It's not actually about trying to force through change, though I'd be very surprised if you didn't witness a single positive impact. It's about what giving a f★★k asks of you as a person. It asks of you every single thing that is listed in this book – and more.

If you want to care, you'll have to keep returning to the present moment, because focusing on the future all the time will blow your head off. Then, after a while, you'll realize just how much pleasure there is to be had, here, in this oft-underrated dimension called right now.

If you care, you'll have to attend to your feelings, because otherwise, my God, will they attend to you. You'll find yourself taking care of your body, and listening to its wisdom, because it allows you to love life with more ease. You'll want to be kind to yourself, and use your imagination to dream of the best things, because anxiety doesn't make you feel good, and it's outlived its use. There's something bigger to plug into. Learn what caring really means, by constantly attending to yourself, and what you need, noting what you do well and what went a bit wrong. Pay attention to each part of your life in turn, and really care about making it feel good.

Before journalism, before coaching, right out of university, I went to the South of France to work as a stewardess on superyachts – those massive gin palaces that sail around the Mediterranean (one had a golf tee on board and another had a submarine). The guests we served were immensely wealthy – I poured drinks, made the beds and ironed the underpants of kings, celebrities, famous business tycoons and political leaders. Millions of euros were spent every day; thrown away as if it were as inconsequential as a toothpick. One lunch-break I was sitting with a weathered deckhand at a port bar, expressing my amazement at the huge amounts of money floating around. He told me that, depending on how long these yacht owners had had their wealth, it altered how they spent it.

'These people get their money and the first thing they do is play. They buy toys. That's what a lot of the people with yachts here are still doing. These are just toys for them.'

He took a long drag of his cigarette, and gestured with his hand to another boat in the harbour, which we knew a famous politician owned.

'Most of them, after a while, they get bored of just having money and playing around, and they want influence, so they go for power instead,' the deckhand told me.

'That's why some of these people are leaders – they go into politics to try and feel better. Or they want fame – that's the other route they take. But the people who have had money for a while, or the people that have real money [in yachting that means billions and billions], they usually go into philanthropy.'

I thought about it, and then went back to the boat to clean up condoms and champagne glasses from the VIP cabin (that guest was still on the play cycle, for sure). However, over ten years later, this conversation has stuck with me. Most of us never reach the immense sums of money that would have us wake up and realize that maybe money isn't everything. We never get to lead a country and realize that doesn't quite hit the spot either. And it takes billions and billions before people wake up and realize that actually, as humans, the thing we want is to do something of value that helps others.

Wouldn't it be great if we didn't need to be superyacht owners before we plugged into the bigger picture? Wouldn't it be great if we could just give a f★★k about who we are, about the world we enmesh with every day, about things in the right order, in the right way. Wouldn't it be great if we could really give a f★★k about each other, right now?

ACKNOWLEDGEMENTS

With thanks to my family and friends, who supported me throughout this process; to Naomi Langan, who helped me edit and shape in the final week before my publisher's deadline, meaning I could meet it on time; and to the One Taste coaching programme and everyone who taught on it – it was the trampoline for the research I did for this book and personal development in general. Thanks also to my editor, Emily Thomas, for being so supportive throughout this process, and to Peter Shiva, who taught me that this moment matters.

NOTES

Yourself

1. This quote is disputed in origin but commonly attributed to Pierre Teilhard de Chardin. It was popularized by Wayne W. Dyer in his talks and Stephen Covey in his book *The 7 Habits of Highly Effective People*, both of whom attribute the words to him.

2. Csikszentmihalyi, M. (1997), *Finding Flow: The Psychology of Engagement with Everyday Life*, New York: Basic Books.

3. Kabat-Zinn, J. (2013), *Full Catastrophe Living*, New York: Bantam Books.

4. Robertson, I. (2018), *The Stress Test*, New York: Bloomsbury.

5. The *Guardian* (2018), '20 amazing facts about the human body'. Available online at: https://www.theguardian.com/science/2013/jan/27/20-human-body-facts-science (accessed 12 June 2018).

6. Parkinson, C. and Lancaster, O. (1958). *Parkinson's Law*. London: John Murray.

7. Manning, Chelsea E. (2018), 'Solitary confinement is "no touch" torture, and it must be abolished', The *Guardian*. Available online at:https://www.theguardian.com/world/commentisfree/2016/may/02/solitary-confinement-is-solitary-confinement-is-torture-6x9-cells-chelsea-manningno-touch-torture-and-it-must-be-abolished (accessed 1 June 2018).

8. Tillisch, K., Labus, J., Kilpatrick, L., Jiang, Z., Stains, J., Ebrat, B., Guyonnet, D., Legrain-Raspaud, S., Trotin, B., Naliboff, B. and Mayer, E.A., 'Consumption of fermented milk product with probiotic modulates brain activity', *Gastroenterology*, 144(7), (2013), pp. 1394–1401.e4.

9. Kuipers, Y., Emonts, M., Ten Brink, P., Mutafoglu, K., Schweitzer, J.-P., Kettunen, M., Twigger-Ross, C., Baker, J., Tyrväinen, L., Hujala, T. and Ojala, A. (2016), 'The Health and Social Benefits of Nature and Biodiversity Protection', a report for the European Commission (ENV.B.3/ETU/2014/0039), Institute for European Environmental Policy, London/Brussels.

10. Bragg, R. and Atkins, G. (2016), 'A Review of Nature-based Interventions for Mental Health Care', Natural England Commissioned Reports, No. 204.

11. Fuentes, A. (2017), *The Creative Spark: How Imagination Made Humans Exceptional*, Penguin.

12. Gamble, C. (2013), *Settling the Earth*, Cambridge, UK: Cambridge University Press.

13. Robinson, Sir K. (Sir Ken of TEDalot on Play and Learning), 'PlayGroundology' (2018). Available online at: https:// playgroundology.wordpress.com/2012/05/06/sir-ken-of-tedalot-on-play-and-learning/ (accessed 31 May 2018).

14. Vohs, K.D., Redden, J.P. and Rahinel, R. (2013), 'Physical order produces healthy choices, generosity, conventionality, whereas disorder produces creativity', *Psychological Science*, 24, 1714–21.

Relationships

15. Ngo, L. et al., (2015) 'Two distinct moral mechanisms for ascribing and denying intentionality', *Scientific Reports*, 5, 17390; doi: 10.1038/srep17390.

16. Zitek, E.M., Jordan, A.H., Monin, B. and Leach, F.R. (2010), 'Victim entitlement to behave selfishly', *Journal of Personality and Social Psychology*, 98(2), 245–55.

17. Brené Brown, YouTube (2018), 'The Power of Vulnerability'. Available online at: https://www.youtube.com/ watch?v=iCvmsMzlF7o&t=194s (accessed 14 June 2018).

18. Hobbes, T. (1904), *Leviathan or The Matter, Forme and Power of a Common Wealth Ecclesiasticall and Civil*, Cambridge, UK: Cambridge University Press.

19. Lieberman, M. (2013), *Social: Why Our Brains are Wired to Connect*, Oxford: Oxford University Press.

20. Nhs.uk. (2018), 'Benefits of Love and Sex' (online). Available at: https://www.nhs.uk/live-well/sexual-health/benefits-of-love-sex-relationships/ (accessed 1 June 2018).

21. Mech, L.D., Adams, L.G., Meier, T.J., Burch, J.W., Dale, B.W. (1998), *The Wolves of Denali*, Minneapolis: University of Minnesota Press.

22. Ziglar, Z. (2012), *Secrets of Closing the Sale*, New York: MJF Books.

23. Maslow, A. (1943), 'A theory of human motivation', *Psychological Review*, 50(4), pp. 370–96.

24. Aesop (2018), *Aesop's Fables*, La Vergne: Dreamscape Media.

25. Burroughs, W. S. (1977), *Junky*, Penguin Books.

26. Carse, J. (1986), *Finite and Infinite Games*, New York: Ballantine Books.

27. Donovan, A. (2016). *Motivate Yourself: get the most out of life, find purpose and achieve fulfilment*, West Sussex, John Wiley & Sons.

28. Osho. (2013). *Fear*. New York: St. Martin's Press.

29. Cacioppo, J.T. and Cacioppo, S. (2014), 'Social relationships and health: the toxic effects of perceived social isolation', *Social and Personality Psychology Compass*.

Infinity and Beyond

30. Taleb, N. and Chandler, D. (2007). *The Black Swan*. Prince Frederick, MD: Recorded Books.

31. Wattles, W. (2017). *The Science of Getting Rich*. La Vergne: Neeland Media LLC.

32. Ames, D. R. and Mason, M. F. (2015) 'Tandem anchoring: informational and politeness effects of range offers in social exchange', *Journal of Personality and Social Psychology*, 108 (2) (February 2015), pp. 254–74.

33. Steptoe, A., Deaton, A. and Stone, A. (2015). 'Subjective wellbeing, health, and ageing'. *The Lancet*, 385(9968), pp.640-648.

34. Lewis, N., Turiano, N., Payne, B. and Hill, P. (2016), 'Purpose in life and cognitive functioning in adulthood, *Aging, Neuropsychology, and Cognition*, 24(6), pp. 662–71.

35. Catto, J. (2017), *Insanely Gifted: Turn Your Demons into Creative Rocket Fuel*, Edinburgh: Canongate Books Ltd.

36. Nepo, M. (2013), *The Little Book of Awakening*, Newburyport, MA: Red Wheel/Weiser.

37. Viscott, D. (2003). *Finding Your Strength in Difficult Times*. New York: McGraw-Hill Education.

38. Dweck, C.S. (2000), *Self-Theories: Their Role in Motivation, Personality, and Development*, Philadelphia: Psychology Press.

39. Molden, D. and Dweck, C. (2006), 'Finding "meaning" in psychology: a lay theories approach to self-regulation, social perception, and social development', *American Psychologist*, 61(3).

40. Chua, H., Boland, J. and Nisbett, R. (2005), 'From the cover: cultural variation in eye movements during scene perception', *Proceedings of the National Academy of Sciences*, 102(35), pp. 12629–33.

41. Bohm, D. (2002), *Wholeness and the Implicate Order*, Hoboken: Routledge.